# The Engaged Organisation

The simple, proven way to
create the engaged company
you dream about

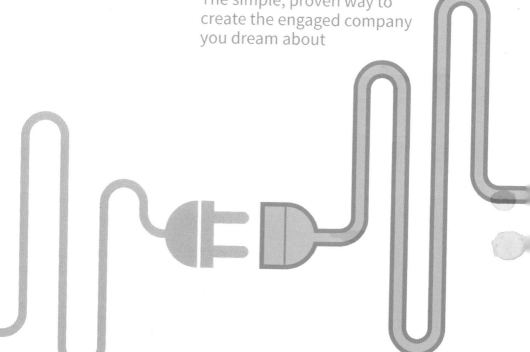

## Stefan Wissenbach
*Founder of Engagement Multiplier*

# Contents

## A Note of Gratitude

### To Dan Sullivan and Babs Smith

On the 24th of June 2013, Dan Sullivan, Babs Smith, and the team at Strategic Coach® hosted a meeting at the Park Hyatt Chicago for over 100 entrepreneurs. The subject: The Self-Managing Company.® I was speaking that afternoon on simple ways to raise engagement levels in business, an important focus for any owner that wants a Self-Managing Company.

After my presentation, Dan suggested I write another book, and *The Engaged Organisation* is the result.

But that's not all I have to thank Dan for.

In 1996, I joined The Strategic Coach Program® — the leading coaching program for entrepreneurs, founded and run by Dan and Babs. It has had a tremendous impact on my life and businesses. I've learned to be a better entrepreneur, and I've made many friends. Every ninety days, I have the opportunity to attend a coaching workshop where I have the pleasure of spending time with entrepreneurs who are building great businesses. It was in a Strategic Coach workshop that I had a business idea that would subsequently become a global exponential company: EngagementMultiplier.com.

Thank you, Dan and Babs, for raising my levels of thinking, for believing in me, and for inspiring me to create and grow Engagement Multiplier®. You witnessed the entrepreneurial journey and, when times got tough, were supportive and wise. I will always be grateful.

You have encouraged me to shoot for the stars and build a business beyond my wildest dreams.

# Engagement

*The electricity that enables everything else to multiply*

Engagement is magical. More specifically, the outcomes delivered by engagement are magical.

In the same way an accomplished magician delivers an extraordinary outcome that delights and astonishes, engagement transforms both lives and businesses from ordinary to extraordinary.

Ever since my teenage years I've been fascinated by the transformational power of engagement, both at a personal and a business level. I've seen how organisations that apply sound engagement principles become market leaders, and positively impact the lives of many. I've seen how, when we become engaged, life becomes more fulfilling and the greatest progress is made.

We're living in the engagement era. The transformational power of engagement is now widely understood, written, and talked about.

It's become a business hot topic. I've written this book because I believe the approaches taken by many consulting firms and businesses to improve engagement don't focus on the right areas, are often too expensive, are too complicated and don't deliver lasting results.

Fundamentally, many engagement programs are simply not engaging!

I believe creating an 'Engaged Organisation' requires:

- An understanding of the elements that make an Engaged Organisation

- The ability to measure and score engagement levels on an ongoing basis

- An understanding of simple engagement principles

- A top-down commitment to engagement

- An ongoing commitment to ensure that engagement becomes part of the organisation's culture

There's a very good reason why the subtitle of this book references the '*Company* You Dream About' — a deliberate play on words. This book can help you create the business you've always dreamt of — one that's easy to run; that seamlessly markets, sells, serves, and makes terrific profits; and that's ultimately saleable (if you want it to be). But of course, 'company' also refers to the people who surround us. In an Engaged Organisation, it's the people who make a business joyful to own and grow. We're surrounded by people who are committed, connected, and engaged. There's harmony and there's energy. They are fabulous 'company'. We spend so much of our time at work, and doing so with engaged people is much more enjoyable.

Great people, great energy, great products and services, and great profitability: Isn't that the business we all want?

This book will show you how to achieve exactly that.

In today's world, you can't afford not to focus on engagement. Engagement is not just a pleasant by-product in a business, but is rather the central cause of all personal and organisational development and expansion. It's the electricity that enables everything else to multiply.

Businesses that embrace engagement take on an energy level that results in consistent improvement and growth and ultimately, in many cases, exponential outcomes.

And yet, *engagement* is one of those words everyone is using but not everyone understands. The purpose of this book is to explain what engagement is, why it matters so much, and how to create it in your organisation.

Here's my definition:

*Engagement is the ability to be present, focused, and energised.*

Wouldn't it be great if that were how everyone in your company felt? What kind of results could you create with a fully engaged team?

When you're engaged, your relationships are stronger, your happiness levels rise, you accomplish more, and you have the power to achieve your most difficult goals. Nowhere is this more evident than in the business world.

Engaged Organisations are easier to run — they make more money, suffer less waste, and are happier places to work.

The evidence is overwhelming, and yet many business owners still resist engagement. Or they dabble (dangerously) in it and then (unfortunately) abandon it, because they haven't quite managed to separate the myths surrounding engagement from the reality. If these reluctant business owners knew the statistics and understood how to set up a foolproof engagement framework, they would change their minds.

Engagement is important to businesses of every sector and size, from those with a handful of employees to those with tens of thousands. However, historically, only larger corporations have woken up to the massive commercial impact of improving engagement. Some of these corporations pay consultants tens of thousands of dollars to come in and try to make engagement happen. Others consult with academic experts, whose recommendations are often filled with technical jargon and theories that cause more confusion than clarity. In both cases, positive results can be difficult to realise.

Frankly, you don't need to pay an expensive consultant or academic expert to borrow your watch and tell you the time.

The keys to turning your organisation into an Engaged Organisation already exist within your business — you just need to know how to find them and use them.

People often don't give enough credit to the expertise and intelligence already available within their own businesses. In my experience, most organisations are full of untapped potential. With the right framework and systems in place, you will be able to understand what your engagement resources are, and how to best utilise them.

I have spent most of my entrepreneurial career providing people and businesses with the necessary structures to fulfil their potential and become sustainably more productive, profitable, and engaged.

By following my recommendations in this short book, you will be able to:

- Understand what makes an Engaged Organisation

- Establish your organisation's 'Engagement Score'

- Identify where you can best focus your resources for maximum benefit

- Create an Engaged Purpose for your organisation

- Engage your leadership in a unified strategy

- Make engagement a priority in your business (and ultimately make it part of your organisation's culture)

- Reduce your staff turnover and increase morale

- Improve your organisational efficiency (and profits!)

And, importantly:

- Experience a sustainable lift in your own level of enthusiasm and engagement!

These results may appear to be too good to be true. Yet history, research, and my own personal experience show that when you adopt the principles in this book, they are *all* attainable — and I will show you how.

In the following chapters, I'll reveal incredibly effective and easy-to-understand engagement tools and strategies that will give you the Engaged Organisation (and company) you dream about. This book will empower you to move your organisation, your team, and your levels of success upward for many years to come.

Here's to your Engaged Organisation, the energy it brings, and a dream realised!

*Stefan Wissenbach*

# Chapter 1

# The Engaged Organisation

*The only four elements you need to master*

*'Begin with the end in mind.'*
—Stephen Covey—

I t is easier to complete a puzzle with a picture of the end result in front of you — and the same is true with an Engaged Organisation. In this chapter, I'm going to share with you what an Engaged Organisation looks like.

An Engaged Organisation is the result of four key elements that work together in a harmonious way. I will explain each of them now, and then I'll address each in detail in the following chapters.

The first and fundamental element of any Engaged Organisation sits at its core — the **Engaged Purpose**.

An Engaged Purpose is a written statement that clearly communicates to your team what your company does and why. It details the transformation you are trying to create.

The purpose emanates from the Engaged Owner — but it absolutely connects with the leaders and employees. It is communicated with passion to those inside and outside the organisation, and it is the most important piece of the puzzle. By connecting all the other parts, the purpose provides both the structure and the clarity that enables the organisation to become engaged.

Provide the 'why' for all the functions within your business, and you will inspire your team members to align their daily activities with this higher purpose.

The next piece of the puzzle is **Engaged Ownership**.

Owners who are passionate about engagement within their organisations will experience its benefits — greater success and satisfaction at work and at home, higher profits, better relationships with employees and customers, and ultimately, a Self-Managing Company® or a business that can be sold (if you want to) for a handsome multiple. Becoming an Engaged Owner requires going the extra mile, but the prize of having the company you've always dreamt about is worth it!

The next piece of the puzzle is **Engaged Leaders**.

I use the term *leaders* instead of *managers*. You might prefer *managers*, *supervisors*, *team leaders*, or something unique to your organisation. Whatever the terminology in your company, when these people embrace the principles of engagement, they can rightfully be called Engaged Leaders.

As an Engaged Owner, it is critical that you build a team of Engaged Leaders. These people play a key part in turning the Engaged Purpose into reality, motivating and energising their teams to do the same. Leaders are essential to the creation of the final crucial piece of this puzzle: Engaged Employees.

**Engaged Employees** sit at the front line.

In most businesses, employees are where engagement meets the outside world. Without Engaged Employees, you will never have an Engaged Organisation.

It's these four essential elements that, when combined, create and *protect* the **Engaged Organisation**. Many engagement programs focus on creating engaged customers, but until a company has cultivated the four component parts I have described, focusing on customers is a mistake.

I can still clearly remember a 'Customer First' engagement program initiated at great cost at the first company I worked at, over 25 years ago. The program did deliver some initial benefits; however, because the organisation neglected to focus on the four critical elements, the results were short lived.

I passionately believe that every business should have an Engaged Purpose, and that engagement should begin as a top-down driven program, with owners and leaders initially taking responsibility. By setting an example for employees and following through on engagement initiatives, you will see the ownership for engagement shifting from being leadership-driven to team-driven.

Connected by a purpose and confident that engagement is supported by leaders and owners (and not just the latest fad), team members will habitually suggest and implement ideas to raise engagement levels and the company's engagement score. The business results will speak for themselves.

In an Engaged Organisation, the owners, leaders, and employees connect with each other around the purpose, protecting the organisation, preserving its values, and driving its growth and profitability.

As the components engage, your Engaged Organisation grows and becomes stronger. With these core elements locked in place, the impact travels — engagement spreads outward from your organisation into the rest of the world.

The energy emanating from an Engaged Organisation is palpable and impacts everyone who comes into contact with the business — not just the customers.

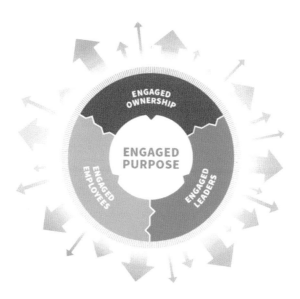

Engagement is contagious. An Engaged Organisation makes an impact on suppliers, consultants and media partners, as well as the families of those who work for the company and even the local community.

So just how engaged is your organisation right now? The way to measure your company's current level of engagement can be found in the next chapter.

# Chapter 2

# What's Your Organisation's Score?

## *If you can measure it, you can improve it*

*'That which is measured improves.*
*That which is measured and reported improves exponentially.'*
—Karl Pearson, founder of the modern field of statistics—

Unless you can measure something, it's very difficult to improve it in a meaningful way. I regularly hear from business owners about how they take engagement seriously and complete many initiatives to improve engagement levels in their organisations. And yet, in most cases, they lack a consistent, reliable, and predictable method by which to evaluate the success of these initiatives and the return on investment in time and money that goes into them. This was one of the key reasons why I created the **Engaged Organisation Scorecard**™. The Scorecard gives you a score for your organisation, but it also gives you much more. It sparks creative, problem-solving thoughts and conversations. Likewise, humans respond best when provided with structure and frameworks within which they have freedom to operate.

In my early conversations with businesses about engagement, I realised very quickly that it was easy for confusion to exist across an organisation when it came to defining what was meant by 'engagement'. Having identified the elements of an Engaged Organisation,

I have been in rooms full of people and watched them silently score themselves. In less than ten minutes, they look up. They look around. They look toward me, and by the expressions on their faces I can see that they've discovered something that has been lurking right under their noses.

I set about defining each of them, based on one of the following four quadrants or organisational states: Dysfunctional, Fragmented, Successful, and Engaged.

I noticed immediately how easy it was for owners, leaders, and employees to position their business on the Scorecard and arrive at a score.

The **Engaged Organisation Scorecard™** is a simple, powerful tool that allows you to measure and continuously improve engagement in your organisation. The Scorecard turns the emotional feeling of engagement into a measurement.

I have been in rooms full of people and watched them silently score themselves. In less than ten minutes, they look up. They look around. They look toward me, and by the expressions on their faces I can see they've discovered something that has been lurking right under their noses. I see a-ha moments. I sense excitement, gratitude, and relief. And almost instantly, I see their realisation — 'I know what I need to do next.'

As soon as you measure the

present-day engagement of your organisation, you will see where you can begin to make improvements. The first time you use the Scorecard, you'll almost certainly notice that your score points to several areas in which you have already been contemplating making changes.

Most people have found the Scorecard to be an immediate game-changer and a long-term pathway to comprehensive, permanent engagement progress in their companies.

As a result of working with over a hundred businesses using the Scorecard, I decided to create an online engagement platform: Engagement Multiplier. This automates the manual process of using the Scorecard, introduces greater confidentiality, and saves time and effort for businesses, owners, and teams. The results are packaged for everyone in the organisation via digital dashboards, delivering additional insight and value. It's a unique and highly effective automated engagement program specifically built for entrepreneurs. More information exists at the end of this chapter and at EngagementMultiplier.com.

## Now It's Time to Score!

There are three ways to discover your score:

### 1. Photocopy and use the Scorecard in this book

### 2. Download and print the Scorecard

### 3. Use Engagement Multiplier

If you're an Engagement Multiplier customer, the scoring process will be completed confidentially online.

If you're using the book's Scorecard, it can be found on page 17.

If you're downloading the Scorecard, it can be found at:

**EngagementMultiplier.com/en-gb/eobook**

If you're using Engagement Multiplier, you can skip the five steps below. Otherwise, here's how I recommend you proceed:

**Step One: Your Score.** It all starts with *you.* The engagement level of your company starts with your own engagement as an entrepreneur or business owner. To obtain the most value from the Scorecard exercise, I recommend that you first complete the Scorecard yourself. Be as honest with yourself as possible.

**Step Two: Your Leadership Score.** After you've scored yourself, ask each member of your leadership to complete the Scorecard. Then meet with them to discuss and compare results. This step is fundamental and usually fun.

You can't build an Engaged Organisation if you can't engage in open dialogue with your leadership team. If you find you get stuck here, set a short-term goal to make the necessary changes to get your team talking. I can't overstate how valuable Step Two is. An honest, open discussion that includes everyone's views about the organisation's current level of engagement will put you on track immediately toward the creation of an aligned view of the present and the future. This simple exercise delivers invaluable insights. And again, you'll find it an unexpected source of energy as you and your team face the truth as never before!

**Step Three: Your Employees' Score.** Once a unified set of scores is settled upon during the leadership meeting, it's time to establish what the rest of the company thinks. Until the exercise is complete, I recommend that you keep any previously defined scores private so that no one is influenced beforehand. There's always the tendency for employees to tell management what they think management wants to hear. In order for this exercise to be really successful, management needs to hear the unvarnished truth — confidentiality is key!

Whilst I recommended that members of the leadership team complete and discuss their scores in an open forum, I recommend that individual team members complete the Scorecard on an anonymous and confidential basis at first, because in my experience this delivers the most accurate results.

I also recommend that you provide team members with the opportunity to confidentially provide feedback and observations. At Engagement Multiplier, our automated survey asks two key questions:

1. What two actions could you personally take in the next ninety days, that aren't dependent on leadership, to improve overall engagement?

2. What one action do you think leadership could take to improve engagement?

Even after seeing thousands of Engagement Multiplier survey responses, I still find myself marvelling at the quality of the team feedback. Remember, confidentiality is key to getting the best results and truth.

People seldom use the feedback mechanism in a silly or unprofessional way. Instead, you find that comments are carefully considered. A mentor once told me, 'When people provide constructive feedback or criticism it's because, at some level, they care. What's more worrying is if they don't provide any feedback, as this can mean they've given up.' That's worth remembering.

**Step Four: Compare Results!** With a set of scores for both the leadership and team in place, you can review, compare, and reflect. The insights into where you are already an Engaged

Organisation — and where you need to improve — will be invaluable. With the scorecard results you will have a roadmap that not only opens up discussion but also makes very clear what needs to be done.

**Step Five: Repeat!** Again, you'll achieve and sustain your Engaged Organisation best if you regularly repeat the process of evaluating your organisation's scores, soliciting insights and feedback, and taking action. You never want to achieve Engaged Organisation status and then rest on your laurels. You will get tremendous value from using the Scorecard the first time, but that value has the potential to grow exponentially if you continue to track how your scores change over time. My recommended frequency is every ninety days, which is the frequency of our automated engagement surveys at Engagement Multiplier.

Keeping engagement at the forefront of everyone's thinking achieves valuable results. I also recommend you redo the scoring exercise after you have completed this book and acted on the insights it has sparked.

## Persistence Prevails When All Else Fails

Before we move on, here is a serious note of caution: *Dabbling with engagement can cause disengagement.* If your team senses this is just a 'flavour of the month' exercise, they'll do what people in most organisations do — play a waiting game until they're certain that you've abandoned your interest in it and moved on to some other shiny thing. The best way to create engagement is to demonstrate your own personal, ongoing commitment to it. Otherwise, your people will perceive the endeavour as hollow and won't take it — or you — seriously.

Commit to a program of engagement. Stick to it. Acknowledge and share successes, and celebrate progress often. Engagement requires bravery. You have to be prepared to listen to feedback and take action.

If, at this point, you feel unprepared to commit yourself and your team to maintaining a focus on engagement, you should pause before taking any action. All too often in business we see the launch of new initiatives with much fanfare and enthusiasm, only to then see the energy drain slowly away. We have seen some of the most promising initiatives grow derelict and forgotten — once lauded but now entirely ignored.

You have to be in the engagement game for the long haul. Remember, some of your team members will immediately embrace the Engaged Organisation program, whilst others will take a bit longer to come around to it, and some will fall off the wagon immediately. Do allow yourself and your team time to reflect on questions, re-evaluate processes, and perhaps even observe some of the benefits of engagement first, before you expect them to fully engage themselves.

Managed properly, you will enjoy some quick wins and experience the benefits of engagement immediately, but remember that evolution doesn't happen overnight. It takes time and ongoing focus to embed a culture of engagement into an organisation. Resist the urge to abandon your engagement efforts when you reach that first plateau — and you *will* reach a plateau. Stick to it. You'll ascend.

I sometimes hear business owners cite a concern about the amount of time it takes to manage an engagement program in the way I suggest and in the way we support businesses at Engagement Multiplier. The reality is that, done properly, the time impact is minimal. And the time gains outweigh the time costs. When teams become more engaged, they become more productive. There's less time wasted. Tasks are completed faster, with more innovation and more energy. To business owners who tell me they can't afford the time, my reply is simple: 'You can't afford to NOT invest the time.'

As soon as you start making moves toward greater engagement within your company, people will take notice. Those who want to be more engaged will plug in and start growing; those who don't will go elsewhere. A bit of Darwinian science is involved with most human change: Those who aren't adaptable enough to engage will fall to the wayside. This is not your loss.

Yes, the world outside your organisation will always continue to change in ways that can't be predicted. But remember, an Engaged Organisation is strong and protected because it is cross-engaged, bonded, and linked together with a strong sense of purpose.

It doesn't serve you to waste a moment's time dwelling on all the imagined disruptive forces that threaten to undermine your engagement efforts. The only thing that can actually prevent you from striving for more engagement is your own unfounded fear. Consider all the reasoning we have presented for the positive outcomes associated with engagement. There is, in fact, more evidence to come.

With that in mind, let's set you up to create a more Engaged Organisation, wherein everyone involved is positively aligned and energised.

Base the future growth of your company on the Scorecard and it won't matter how the world changes. You and your organisation will always be improving, and therefore capable of meeting those unexpected challenges.

## The Magic of Mastery

In the Introduction, I referenced how a great magician delivers an exceptional outcome when he performs a series of practised moves in front of an audience. A great magic trick dazzles whilst remaining a mystery to the observer. To the outsider, your Engaged Organisation may appear to work just like a magic trick. Those on the outside can't explain what is happening before their very eyes, nor do they believe they can duplicate the results.

But they can.

Great magicians achieve results through persistent practice. What appears to be magic is actually *mastery*, not mystery And mastery delivers exceptional outcomes.

When business leaders establish their organisations' need for more engagement, and then practise, repeat, and master the 'moves' of engagement, the result is the same kind of exceptional outcome that delights the magician's audience.

And it feels magical.

## The Engaged Organisation Scorecard™

|  | DYSFUNCTIONAL | FRAGMENTED | SUCCESSFUL | ENGAGED | SCORE |
|---|---|---|---|---|---|
|  | 1  2  3 | 4  5  6 | 7  8  9 | 10  11  12 |  |
| **ENGAGED PURPOSE** | No Purpose, No Direction | Not Shared, Not Used | General Awareness | Clear, Shared, Connected |  |
| **ENGAGED OWNERSHIP** | Trapped, Reactive, Overwhelmed | No Plan, No System | Closely Held Goals | Visionary Leadership |  |
| **ENGAGED LEADERS** | Self-Centred Survival | Competing, Conflicting, Silos | Operational Execution | Growth Integrators |  |
| **ENGAGED EMPLOYEES** | Shut Down, Fearful | Unmotivated, Minimum Effort | Satisfactory, Impersonal | Personal-Teamwork Alignment |  |
| **ENGAGED CUSTOMERS** | Suspicious, Adversarial | Commoditised, Disposable | Productive, Conventional Relations | Everything Grows, Everybody Wins |  |

EngagementMultiplier™

| NAME | | DATE | SCORECARD TOTAL | /60 |
|---|---|---|---|---|

# The Engaged Organisation Scorecard™

| | | DYSFUNCTIONAL | | | FRAGMENTED | | |
|---|---|---|---|---|---|---|---|
| | | 1 | 2 | 3 | 4 | 5 | 6 |
| **ENGAGED** | **PURPOSE** | **No Purpose, No Direction** Non-existent or woefully out of date, the purpose is an inaccurate document that is never referenced and bears no relevance to the organisation's strategic direction, goals, and business activities. Without an effective core purpose, business activity is disorganised and inefficiency is commonplace. | | | **Not Shared, Not Used** A written purpose that is occasionally referred to by the senior team, but not often updated or utilised to drive strategic direction and business activities. It is not shared with the whole organisation, and as a result, most employees are unaware of the business's overall purpose and goals. | | |
| **ENGAGED** | **OWNERSHIP** | **Trapped, Reactive, Overwhelmed** Ownership feels trapped in reactive attempts to deal with cash flow, debt, and credit crises. As a result, they're disengaged from daily activities. Ownership doesn't care about the well-being of their workforce, nor recognise or appreciate their efforts. They value technology over people and aren't excited about their organisation's future. | | | **No Plan, No System** Owners are minimal, short-range goal setters, with no system for measuring achievement beyond financial results. They have few or no mechanisms in place to create an Engaged Organisation, because they don't truly understand the power of engagement and its impact. They view success purely in financial terms and don't 'know' their people and the true potential they can offer the organisation. | | |
| **ENGAGED** | **LEADERS** | **Self-Centred Survival** Due to the organisation's financial crises, leaders are forced into short-term survival strategies. They do not give or receive regular feedback, rarely conduct scheduled review meetings, and are not genuinely interested in team members' well-being. Leaders lack autonomy and responsibility to turn purpose into action. They often use their status to further only their own interests and have high staff turnover within their teams. | | | **Competing, Conflicting, Silos** Leaders plan and operate with a few business goals they focus on to maintain and improve upon their organisational status and rewards. They provide sporadic feedback to team members, but it is viewed as a necessary (but not rewarding) part of their role. They are only interested in employees performing their roles to satisfaction rather than their happiness and achievements. | | |
| **ENGAGED** | **EMPLOYEES** | **Shut Down, Fearful** 'A Players' are already gone, and remaining employees are hanging onto their jobs from one pay cheque to the next. They operate with a blame culture and are simply going through the motions by doing the minimum possible to get the job done. They do not engage or communicate with team members or leaders, nor do they set goals. They have no energy or passion for their work. | | | **Unmotivated, Minimum Effort** Employees are largely disengaged from both the purpose and goals of the organisation beyond ensuring continued job security and promotion. They usually work to the required standard and see their job as a means to pay bills, but no more. They may have some short-term personal goals, but they are not written down or shared with their colleagues or leaders. They're taking no proactive action to achieve them. | | |
| **ENGAGED** | **CUSTOMERS** | **Suspicious, Adversarial** Relationships with customers are negative, time-consuming, and strained. The best customers are long gone, and those remaining withhold payment and constantly complain. Customers view their relationships with the organisation as short term and commit minimum effort and focus on protecting only their own interests. The organisation is considered difficult to deal with, and relationships feel like hard work, energy-zapping, and counter-productive. | | | **Commoditised, Disposable** The organisation fails to attract the best customers. Relationships with existing customers are run-of-the-mill, fickle, and price sensitive. Opportunities to grow the business relationship to the benefit of both the organisation and the customer are often missed. There's a lack of innovative thinking and mediocrity is the norm. | | |

EngagementMultiplier™

# The Engaged Organisation Scorecard™

| SUCCESSFUL | | | ENGAGED | | | |
|---|---|---|---|---|---|---|
| 7 | 8 | 9 | 10 | 11 | 12 | SCORE |
| **General Awareness** A written purpose that is kept up-to-date and usually referred to when driving strategy, direction, and business activities. The written purpose is shared with most people within the business so they are aware of the purpose, where to find it, and the role they play in supporting it. | | | **Clear, Shared, Connected** A clearly articulated, living, breathing, written purpose shared with every member of the business. It is regularly used and updated as context for creating a sustainable business model, whilst driving strategy, direction, and business activities the leadership has confidence in. Everyone in the business feels connected to and excited by the organisation's ultimate purpose, goals, and how the business will achieve them. Relationships with the organisation's customers are aligned with and support the purpose. | | | |
| **Closely Held Goals** These are committed goal-setting owners, but share their goals with only a few individuals. They have some mechanisms in place to help their organisation progress and develop, and offer fair reward and recognition to their teams. They take some time to get to know people in their organisation and are open-minded to the power of engagement. | | | **Visionary Leadership** Ownership has written plans for its own future and a purpose it's passionate about. They embrace change and innovation and are on a forward trajectory. Ownership shares their inspiration and motivation. They are genuinely concerned about their employees, actively encouraging them to fulfil their own potential. They lead by example and are passionate about creating an Engaged Organisation. | | | |
| **Operational Execution** Leaders support the goals of the owners and organisation, but communicate only within the framework of the organisation's operating and growth structures. They often give and receive team member feedback and conduct planned reviews that are purely focused on business objectives at least once per year. They have some knowledge of engagement, but don't always have a system in place to effectively apply that knowledge. | | | **Growth Integrators** Leaders are passionate about the organisation's goals. They break down barriers, putting people first by getting to know them, showing appreciation, and encouraging a culture of self-improvement. They feel connected to ownership and empowered to proactively translate purpose into action. Leaders engage in effective, regular communication and feedback with team members and conduct open, two-way reviews on at least a quarterly basis. | | | |
| **Satisfactory, Impersonal** Employees are engaged with the organisation's success goals. They contribute to team activities when asked and proactively prepare for annual reviews, sometimes actively seeking feedback on an ongoing basis. They feel their organisation supports their professional growth and that their leaders are supportive. They have confidence in the business's leadership and direction and generally enjoy coming to work. | | | **Personal-Teamwork Alignment** Employees, inspired by the goals of ownership and leaders, use their progress and success in the workplace as a foundation for greater personal futures. They understand how their role contributes to the organisation's success, often suggesting improvements to enhance either their own performance or that of the business. They enjoy trusting, open communication with their leaders and bring their "whole selves" to work. | | | |
| **Productive, Conventional Relations** The organisation as a whole attracts and cultivates successful, growth-oriented customers and provides excellent products and services to them. Interaction with customers is business-like and successful, but sometimes lacks fun, inspiration and '10X thinking'. | | | **Everything Grows, Everybody Wins** The organisation cares about its customers and passionately, abundantly, and contagiously multiplies its 'goals culture' to positively impact relationships with them. It attracts proactive, positive feedback, and customers go the extra mile to nurture the relationship, regularly providing referrals and, in turn, become more engaged themselves. Interaction is enjoyable, productive, energising, and often doesn't feel like work. | | | |
| NAME / DATE / SCORECARD TOTAL | | | | | | /60 |

Chapter 3

# Facts and Myths

*Why engagement is critical
to the success of your business*

*'The facts fairly and honestly presented;
the truth will take care of itself.'*
—William Allen White, *Sage of Emporia*—

Still need some convincing about the power of engagement?

When we are fully engaged with the task at hand, we are more aware, more active, and more focused on what we're doing. When we are not engaged, we go through the motions, and we don't give the task our undivided attention.

Think of what happens when you're watching a big game and you're an avid, enthusiastic fan of one of the teams. You cheer when your team scores, you shout at the referee when your team is penalised, and you pound your fists on the table when the other team scores. You are engaged with what you're observing — maybe so much that others observing your behaviour think you're nuts!

Now think about the experience of watching a game if you don't really care about either team. You love the sport, so you've turned the game on, but as it goes on, you find yourself easily distracted. If someone were to ask you the score, you might not even know. Your mind may drift elsewhere, or you may get so bored you end up falling asleep on the couch.

In the first instance, you're completely involved and excited about every play made in that game. In the second instance, you are barely aware of what's happening. Yet in both cases, the sport on the screen is the sport you love. What's the difference?

The difference is your *level of engagement*.

This same principle applies to the people who work for you. They could be totally passionate about their jobs — watching for every pass, every interference call, every fumble — or they could be uninterested and easily distracted.

They could even be napping during the game!

Most likely, your team lies somewhere between these extremes. But one thing is painfully obvious: The lower the engagement level of your organisation, the lower your people's productivity and motivation. The leader of a *disengaged* organisation is caught in a downward spiral, and he often feels little hope. This lack of passion and energy filters into every aspect of the business, and thus becomes a self-perpetuating cycle.

The business and the individuals working in it become trapped in survival mode. Whilst the owner frets about making payroll and paying bills, the disengaged employees do the minimum amount of work. They feel no motivation to work harder, smarter, or faster.

The evidence supporting the power of engagement is overwhelming. Here is just an example:

> **According to the Corporate Leadership Council, Engaged Organisations grow profits up to three times faster than their competitors. They also report that highly engaged companies are able to reduce staff turnover by eighty-seven percent.[1]**

The evidence is indisputable: Engagement helps you make more

---

1 *'Driving Performance and Retention Through Employee Engagement'*, Corporate Leadership Council Executive Summary, 2004

money — a *lot* more. It also helps you retain the valued team members who are critical to helping you realise those profits. Study after study shows that Engaged Organisations hire for growth, rather than just to maintain the status quo. Engaged Organisations look forward, and their team members look forward to coming to work.

Now, contrast that with this shocker of a statistic:

**Eighty-seven percent of workers around the world are NOT engaged with their jobs.**[2]

Sadly, **almost nine out of ten workers** don't care much about what they do as long as they get paid, according to the most recent Gallup worldwide business study.

How many of these disengaged individuals work for you? Worse still, how many of them come to your workplace each morning and barely work at all?

Most businesses are *not realising their full potential — and they don't even know it.*

Note how workers who are not engaged compare to workers who are:

- Engaged employees working remotely without a supervisor actually *work more hours at their jobs* than do those who are on site but not engaged.

- According to Gallup, an Engaged Organisation enjoys an overwhelming host of benefits, including fewer sick days, higher employee retention, higher profits, higher productivity, fewer job-related accidents, fewer quality errors, better customer service, and higher customer loyalty.

Every business owner understands the importance of hiring the

2 Gallup report, *State of the Global Workplace*

right people, and yet statistics show that the disengagement problem is costing the US economy alone *$450 billion to $550 billion per year.*[3] Furthermore, the average cost of replacing a disengaged employee runs up to 213 percent of his or her salary.[4] Clearly, you can bring on all the right people and organise all the right teams, but if you fail to engage them, you'll have spent your time and money unwisely.

Groups are at their most powerful when members are fully engaged. When individuals align strongly with their organisation's purpose, they are invested in that organisation's productivity. These are the people who leap out of bed every morning and show up ready, willing, and able. The 2014 *State of the American Workplace* Gallup poll I referenced a moment ago reported that:

- **The top twenty-five percent of engaged companies have significantly higher productivity, profitability, and customer ratings; less turnover and absenteeism; and fewer safety incidents than those in the bottom twenty-five percent;**

- **Those businesses with more engaged workers also experienced 147 percent higher earnings per share (EPS) compared to their competition.**

Gallup has conducted an employee engagement assessment every two to four years since the 1990s, analysing data from hundreds of organisations in dozens of industries worldwide. Every year, studying over one million employees, they confirm there is a well-established connection between employee engagement and job performance.

Engagement is proven to have a much greater effect on your employees' well being than company benefits — it drives performance more than do the fanciest company policies or perks. Leaders who focus on their

---

3 2014 Gallup report, *State of the American Workplace*
4 Center for American Progress

employees' strengths can practically eliminate disengagement and *double* the average level of employee engagement in their organisations.

Engage people and they'll become happier. Happier people will engage more enthusiastically, and you will have created a 'virtuous circle' — the opposite of the vicious circle about which we've all heard so much.

When organisations become engaged, they see happiness levels rise. When engagement levels rise, efficiency and profits rise, too. Growth becomes easier. The multinational business management consultant firm Accenture found that organisations that invested just another ten percent in engagement initiatives increased their profits by **$2,400 per employee — that's about £2,000.**

So if a lack of engagement is so perilous, why doesn't everyone automatically flock to create engagement initiatives?

If hundreds of studies have proven that engagement is effective, why have so many business owners not yet grasped its importance or taken action to improve engagement levels in their businesses?

I think it's because the consulting firms specialising in engagement are focused on the larger corporations. Smaller businesses, typically those with fewer than 500 employees, are poorly supported when it comes to strategies to measure and improve engagement. They often have great legal, financial, and accounting advisors but don't have anyone to help them with engagement. In my experience, even small to medium-sized businesses benefit significantly from focusing on engagement.

I've also noticed that business owners believe a number of myths about engagement. It's worth us discussing three of the most prevalent ones.

## Three Engagement Myths

### Myth #1: Engagement is a nicety, not a necessity!

Many business owners (particularly in the up-to-500-employee group) say, 'Engagement is all very well, but I'm not sure it would make much of a difference in my business if we focused on it. My staff seems happy enough and the business is running well. It's a *nice* to have rather than a *need* to have.'

Oh, how wrong they are.

To begin with, most businesses have no idea how engaged their people are because they have no way of measuring it. My extensive experience measuring employee engagement — both with the Scorecard and with EngagementMultiplier.com — shows that, in the majority of cases, actual employee engagement levels differ from the levels perceived by the owners.

The Engaged Organisation Scorecard not only lets you measure engagement, it shows you what better engagement looks like and how to get there. If you provide the right structure and framework, you'll improve your company's engagement level — and quickly realise that doing so is a necessity, not a nicety.

Take the example of Fabick CAT, a company with more than 600 employees headquartered in the US. Fabick CAT sells, rents, and repairs Caterpillar construction equipment.

Back in 1999, when Doug Fabick took over the company from his father, he decided to assess the company's engagement level.

The initial diagnosis was pretty dire: A study of Fabick's workforce indicated that only sixteen percent — one in six employees — could be described as engaged.

Having studied engagement research, Fabick firmly believed that increasing this percentage would pump serious profit back into the company's system. Over the next seven years, the company put $500,000 into engagement initiatives designed to help team members connect more strongly with their work roles. The end result was phenomenal. Whilst overall revenues increased by fifteen percent, actual profits increased by **100 percent** because of added efficiency savings — bringing in *an extra $3 million* to the company and a whopping *600 percent ROI* on that

$500,000 investment![5]

The good news is that you don't have to spend large sums to improve engagement. You don't have to be a large company with a huge bank balance to implement change. The truth is, with this book, you have everything you need to become an Engaged Owner, running an Engaged Organisation full of Engaged Leaders and Teams who take care of Engaged Customers.

## Myth #2: If you want employees to be happy, just give them more money!

When it comes to career satisfaction and money, there is one huge misunderstanding about what matters most:

- A full **eighty-nine percent** of employers believe workers leave to make more money, when in reality…

- Only **twelve percent** of employees leave for that reason![6]

It makes you wonder why the other eighty-eight percent of employees leave, doesn't it?

Engagement does *not* grow simply as a result of a higher pay cheque. Think about all the athletes who earn eight-figure salaries, only to prove to be total busts! Alas, the same phenomenon happens in the business world (albeit with fewer zeros on the cheques).

According to the HR consulting company Towers Watson, the single most important driver of engagement is the extent to which people believe that senior management *has a sincere interest in their well-being*. When you demonstrate that you care, you acquire something money can't buy.

Here's another indication that engagement is about more than just money: According to a poll conducted by *Parade Magazine* in 2012, about

---

5 Jennifer Robison, 'A Caterpillar Dealer Unearths Employee Engagement', *Gallup Business Journal*, October 12, 2006
6 Leigh Branham, *The 7 Hidden Reasons Employees Leave*, AMACOM Books, 2012

thirty-five percent of American workers would turn down a big pay rise in favour of getting the chance to see their supervisor fired instead! That points to a widespread engagement problem. If more supervisors and people at the top knew how to engage, I'm certain the percentage of employees wishing them ill would drop drastically.

That's not to say that people don't appreciate being paid at a fair rate. Of course it's essential to be paid well to do what you love and what you're great at. But positive engagement *trumps money* in most employees' minds, and more businesses must recognise that and act on it.

### Myth #3: Employees don't care about engagement.

This myth is often cited alongside the idea that money is what motivates people to come to work.

In fact, most employees want to be engaged. It's *disengaging organisations* that create disengaged employees.

Dr. Jim Harter, Chief Scientist of Workplace Management and Wellbeing at Gallup, has studied corporate culture for more than twenty-eight years, investigating why so many people feel disengaged in the workplace. His key finding: 'Most people come to work well intentioned and only turn sour when their basic needs aren't being met. You have to get the basics right if you want great engagement.'

Imagine what you can do if you focus on that word 'basic' and take it up a few notches. When you implement the basics of engagement, the good intentions that new employees arrive with not only remain good — they get even better.

Most people these days have dedicated a significant amount of time and money to earning their university degrees, or have set aside resources for continuing education and self-improvement in their careers. Most people have carefully chosen their careers so that what they do on a daily basis and where they spend the majority of their time *matters* to them.

In order to squash Myth #3, we must become like the teacher who assumes on the first day of school that everyone in class is capable of earning an A. Assume the best of your employees and put structures in place to continually engage them, because they are coming to you seeking exactly that (even if they don't initially know it).

All evidence points to the fact that Engaged Organisations are better, more successful, and easier to run. You were drawn to this book for a reason: Engagement matters to you, and you know it begins with you. You are most likely already working in a successful and at least partly engaged environment — but because you are always striving for greatness, you know there is more, and you want it.

When you embrace engagement, you not only benefit from a business that's easier to manage, you become known as a business owner who inspires and attracts the best talent. In the process of becoming more fully engaged, you develop a team that delivers outstanding results — not because they have to, but because they *want* to.

The successful Engaged Owner has set into place a framework that runs flawlessly *because of its people*. When people are engaged, the business moves from strength to strength. Finances run smoothly and well, but that is almost beside the point. Engaged Owners don't just build a business up in order to sell it for a pile of money. Passion and lifestyle motivate them, and that trickles down. Engaged Owners care about the lives and goals of the people they have working with them, and when the employees know this, everyone becomes motivated to give 110 percent.

The facts point to this essential truth: Engagement is critical to the lifeblood of a business.

Let's now look in more detail at each of the elements that make an Engaged Organisation.

Chapter 4

# Engaged Purpose

*The core of your Engaged Organisation*

*'He who has a why to live for can bear almost any how.'*
—Friedrich Nietzsche—

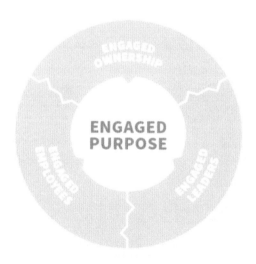

An Engaged Purpose is the core of the Engaged Organisation. It is the glue that holds everything together. It connects your team, provides structure, and appeals to the right customers. It makes growing a business and the people within it so much easier. It simplifies difficult decisions and makes an uncertain future easier to navigate. Having an Engaged Purpose invariably results in a business making more money, but it also provides a reason for that business that goes beyond money.

> An Engaged Purpose is a written statement that clearly communicates to your team what your company does and why. It details the transformation you are trying to create. It provides a structure that will inspire your team to align their daily activities with your company's larger aspirations.

Just like *engagement*, you often hear the terms *vision* and *mission*. I have consistently found in discussions with my clients, however, that neither *vision* nor *mission* means as much as they should. *Purpose* goes deeper than *vision* or *mission*.

Many purpose, mission, or vision statements are written for the organisation's customers. This is wrong. Most customers don't care. They choose to deal with you for reasons other than some words about why you exist and what you do. The people who matter are your team. Write it for them, engage them, and Engaged Customers will be a by-product. (But write it so a customer who wants to read it will enjoy doing so.)

Vision, which can be defined as 'preparation for the future', is useful, but often quite factual — it doesn't necessarily connect to people's emotions. A mission might be described as any work we believe it is our duty to do.

I believe that most missions and visions are too broad and cover too much territory. Workers think locally — and therein lies the disconnect. Often, missions and visions are so grandiose that they confuse or even confound the employees in charge of turning them into reality. That's why I stress the importance of purpose: *why* you do something or *why* something exists. *When you create a big enough 'why' for people, they will become emotionally involved in finding a 'how'.* Purpose is motivational. A compelling purpose touches the heart, not just the head. If you want to rally the troops, purpose should be at the core of everything you do and say.

According to a recent EY (formerly Ernst and Young) survey: Purpose-driven organisations are believed to have better results across a variety of measures:

- **Eighty-nine percent of participants say they encourage greater employee satisfaction;**

- **Eighty-five percent say better customer advocacy; and**

- **Eighty-one percent say higher-quality products and services.**

Study after study has shown that money is low on the list of reasons why people want to come to work. But in a business without a purpose, it's difficult for team members to become engaged — and so employment becomes about the money. Conversely, businesses that have an Engaged Purpose enjoy the benefits of having a team that isn't just in it for the money — and as a result, business success is easier to achieve.

And it is the whole team that needs to be engaged. The owner of a successful business may have articulated a brilliant and clearly defined purpose, yet seldom does that purpose make it to all levels of the organisation. You may have devised the best purpose in the history of humankind, but if it is locked up in an ivory tower and not making it down to the front line, you are hampering your organisation's ability to perform at its full potential.

To the extent that you want to create an Engaged Organisation, you have to find a way to define your purpose and make sure everyone connects with it. The good news is that creating an Engaged Purpose is both straightforward and fun!

Let me now define purpose, break it down into its components, and provide you with the context, structure, and framework to create your own.

## What Makes an Engaged Purpose?

An Engaged Purpose is:

- A clearly articulated, living, breathing, written statement

- Shared with every member of the business

- Regularly updated as context for creating and maintaining a sustainable business model

- Used to drive strategy, direction, and business activities that leadership has confidence in

- A connection between everyone in the business and the organisation's purpose, goals, and strategy

- Aligned with customer relationships

Let's take each in turn.

### A clearly articulated, living, breathing, written statement

By 'clearly articulated', I mean that the purpose is something that any member of the organisation could discuss with family at the dinner table. No one should be bored (not even the teenagers!), and everyone should 'get it'. Purpose is not lofty, esoteric, or highbrow philosophical. When someone starts talking about it — at work, at home, on the train, in fact anywhere — a conversation should naturally follow. You've absolutely nailed it if a new hire is talking to their friends at the end of their first week, gets asked what the business does, replies with your Engaged Purpose, and the response is: 'That sounds like a cool company!'

Unfortunately to the contrary, far too many organisations throw away tens of thousands of pounds on expensive consultants who come up with impressive-sounding but overblown purpose statements. These statements sound fantastic and elicit nods of approval around the marketing table, yet they fail to translate into tangible context and actions for the people within the business. If your employees don't understand your purpose or connect with it, they won't engage with it, no matter how much it costs you to have it worded.

You want an Engaged Purpose that people are proud of.

FedEx's 'The World On Time' is a perfect example of an Engaged Purpose that provides clear guidance. One of the original founders of FedEx once told me a story about a time when the company had just launched and was vulnerable. A FedEx customer had called the office in tears — her wedding was the following day, and her dress hadn't reached her. It had been misdirected somehow and was tracked to another location. The bride-to-be was beside herself.

With absolute clarity, the FedEx employee told the woman not to worry and that she would have the dress in time for her wedding. The employee put down the phone and promptly chartered a light aircraft to fly the dress to the distraught bride — 'The World On Time'.

Now, in case you're gasping in horror at the unauthorised expense of chartering a whole plane to deliver one dress, consider this: Unknown to that employee, present at the wedding was an influential guest in the process of considering a substantial contract with FedEx. Upon hearing of the bride's experience, the guest promptly awarded FedEx his contract.

The stakes may not always be this high, and the results may not always be this remarkable, but FedEx will always aim for the right thing being done. They are a business that empowers its team members to take action through an Engaged Purpose: 'The World On Time'.

It's easy to write a purpose down and then stick it in a drawer and return to business as usual. If a purpose is to be living and breathing, however, it needs to connect powerfully with everything the business is doing or planning to do.

**Shared with every member of the business**

Sharing is not as simple as stating your purpose in your company brochure or on your website. You don't just stamp it on collateral to hand to your new hires on their first day of work. Your purpose should be discussed regularly and actively referred to in team meetings and reviews. It should be visually prominent and officially celebrated every now and again. It should be shared in the most direct way possible — ideally through personal interaction. Be open and honest about your rationale. Encourage your team to ask questions about it — and answer every one. Share your purpose passionately and wholeheartedly.

**Regularly used and updated as context for creating and maintaining a sustainable business model; used to drive strategy, direction, and business activities leadership has confidence in**

It's important to keep your purpose alive even if you don't change it. In other words, from time to time, ensure that the purpose is relevant, engaging, and connecting your team.

Businesses evolve over time. There are countless examples of substantial companies that started as small organisations. As they grew, they moved into different markets, providing different products and services. The very basis of the business today might be different from what it was when the business started. Take some of the larger stores that started by selling fruit and vegetables. They still do that, but they now provide banking, insurance, and many other services to customers. My own business has evolved from just providing strategic consultancy for individual business owners to providing a platform to help entire organisations all over the world become more engaged. We accept that in a successful business (and if your business is engaged, it will be successful) you are going to experience growth and change. It's therefore important that you regularly review your purpose to ensure it is aligned with how the business is evolving and how you want to evolve further.

That said, the purpose must be clearly defined so that it can be used when considering strategy, direction, and business activities. This simple check-and-balance exercise is very useful to go through periodically with the key people in your business.

## A connection between everyone in the business and the organisation's purpose, goals, and strategy

Without an Engaged Purpose, the only reason team members come to work is to get paid, and we have already discussed how trying to initiate engagement based on money alone does not work. You need to present people with a *reason* for wanting to come to work every day.

The best way for me to illustrate this point is to share with you the Engaged Purpose at Engagement Multiplier:

*A More Engaged World …*

*We enable businesses with brave, caring, identifiable ownership to measurably improve morale, culture, and retention and innovate, thrive, and grow.*

*We are deeply connected to, and energised by, the transformational power of 'engagement' for both businesses and individuals.*

*We are proud and protective ambassadors of our community, philosophy, and culture where personal growth and unique ability are championed, collaboration is constant and fun is a priority!*

What we do:

We help create Engaged Organisations — any business in any part of the world.

Why we do it:

Because it's transformative. It reduces employee turnover, increases profits, and makes businesses happier places to work. Every member of our team understands this, and we consistently focus on internally sharing the successes our clients are enjoying. The team is totally connected to the benefits of what we do and therefore appreciate the 'why'.

How we do it:

We proudly harness the power of technology to deliver exponential results for ourselves and our customers.

The result is a purpose that reflects what I am passionate about and something my team is connected to.

When Paul O'Neill took over a struggling Alcoa, he didn't make his company's purpose to be the most profitable supplier of aluminium or other metals. Instead, he announced that his purpose was to eliminate industrial accidents. The uproar from shareholders was enormous. 'How about making money?' they cried. But his commitment to zero industrial accidents energised and united the workforce, which led to countless innovations that not only prevented injuries and saved lives, but also saved money and had a powerful effect on overall profitability. This was a purpose to be reckoned with! What, may I ask, is yours?

## Aligned with customer relationships

Do you treat your customers with the reverence they deserve? After all, plenty of competitors would love to woo them away! Before he became a famous business author, Harvey Mackay ran a paper company. He would send workers to follow his competitors' delivery trucks, and then his sales force would call on those customers. The only reason Mackay's company was able to wrestle those customers from their previous paper suppliers was that those other companies didn't revere them. Mackay not only offered better prices, he put together a filing system that kept track of birthdays, anniversaries, and other special facts about his customers. He maintained and made frequent use of that database, making his customers feel connected to his company. These weren't just price-sensitive, one-time buyers; they were Engaged Customers. Can you say the same thing about yours?

You may only need to create a single, one-size-fits-all purpose, or you may need to break your purpose down into levels. In organisations with fewer than 100 team members, it's usually sufficient to focus on one purpose to create engagement. In larger organisations, it may be advisable to create a purpose for each of the different departments or divisions within your business.

Creating departmental or divisional purposes provides team members with structure and context, enabling them to align their engagement and activities with the larger company vision. In my experience, larger organisations are at high risk of having team members at the front line who are not engaged. Often, this occurs because those team members are only remotely connected to the company's purpose, or disconnected from it entirely.

## FIVE GOLDEN RULES TO HELP YOU CREATE YOUR OWN ENGAGED PURPOSE

1. **Stay true to yourself** — Be mindful of why you started your company in the first place, what you do, and why you do it. A purpose is not meant to change the structure you have in place; it's meant to state what you do and why. Remember the rationale for why you got in the business. Why your industry? Why your location? What void did you see yourself filling? These thoughts connect the functional parts of your business with the emotional reasons for being in it.

2. **Seek the input of the people you want to engage: your team** — Don't fall into the trap of feeling you have to write it yourself. The best results often come from working with your leaders and team to create a compelling and engaging purpose. If they are involved in creating the statement, they're much more likely to own it.

3. **Make it connect** — A unified purpose is written with energy and passion. It robustly expresses what you are

looking to achieve and why. It needs to be a compelling and well-thought-out communication that will touch the hearts and heads of employees at every level.

4.  **Create confidence, belief, and empowerment** — Your purpose should be something that you, the owner, are energised by and truly believe you can attain. It should be authentic. You should feel comfortable discussing it and supporting it. From a team perspective, it should be empowering. You'll be amazed at the truly extraordinary things your team can accomplish when empowered.

5.  **Write clearly, and let it evolve** — The objective should not be to condense the purpose into as few words as possible. All too often the focus is on brevity, when it should be on clarity. A page of copy that connects with and engages your team is far more valuable than a few words that don't. That said, keep it to the point.

---

### Engaged Organisation Action: How Did You Score?

If you're using the Engagement Multiplier Program, you will have already seen how you've scored and the direction you should be taking to improve your score further.

If you're using the book or downloaded Scorecard, go to EngagementMultiplier.com/en-gb/eobook for advice and guidance on actions you can consider taking to improve your score.

---

Armed with an Engaged Purpose, you have the most important thing you need to be an Engaged Owner. That's what we'll move onto next. It's time to talk about *you*!

# Chapter 5

# Engaged Ownership

*You — the Chief Engagement Officer*

*'To win in the marketplace you must first win in the workplace.'*
—Doug Conant, former CEO of Campbell's Soup—

ngagement starts at the top — it starts with you. Whether your organisation consists of you and ten other people or you and a thousand other people, it's your responsibility as the owner to be engaged.

Most organisations *can* function with a small number of disengaged employees. In fact, the evidence shows that most do. When disengagement exists in leaders, however, the impact is often substantial. A disengaged owner can quickly kill a business. And you can't fake it till you make it. You are either engaged or you're not.

An Engaged Owner has three key responsibilities:

1. **Ultimate ownership of the creation and maintenance of the purpose alongside a vision for the business;**

2. **Connecting the leaders to the purpose and vision; and**

3. **Being the organisation's CEO — which in my world means the 'Chief Engagement Officer'.**

If a Chief Executive Officer is sometimes above it all and inaccessible, a Chief Engagement Officer is the opposite: alert, relentlessly involved, and part of the fabric of the organisation.

The Chief Engagement Officer is someone who is passionate about engagement. They understand that it's the electricity that powers the business and are committed to pursuing it as part of the organisation's culture and basis for operation. Engagement is not something they see as being a short-term fad — something that, once attained, can be ignored. They see it as an ongoing, evolving, multiplying process.

The CEO is passionate about the organisation's purpose and has a vision. Such leaders care about what the business does and the well-being of people within their organisation. They understand that people don't just come to work to get paid.

In engagement (as in all things) you set the standard. Whether your culture runs on peaceful coexistence, paranoia, or something in between, your people will model their behaviour on yours. So if you want engagement to be an ever-present, ever-growing, evergreen element in your organisation, the responsibility falls squarely on your shoulders. Think of an Engaged Owner as a maestro conducting an orchestra — your people look to you to lead from the front, pull everyone together, and unify them around your Engaged Purpose.

Many years ago, I was talking with my grandfather about business. The company I worked for at the time was in turmoil. Back then, I didn't understand the power of an Engaged Organisation. My grandfather said to me, 'Stefan, always remember that the fish rots from the head.' I asked him what he meant. He said, 'If you buy a fish and leave it out, it starts to decay, and it rots from the head first — it's the same in business.' As an owner, it's your responsibility not to let rot creep into your organisation so that it turns into a stinking fish!

Don't see the role of Chief Engagement Officer as a daunting, over-whelming task. Get it right, and as your organisation becomes more engaged, your team will take much of the responsibility for improving your organisation's engagement levels. But, until they do, it's up to you.

Of course, most business owners love their businesses, so they accept this responsibility with joy. I hope you will do the same, especially when you understand that engagement doesn't have to be boring — in fact, quite the opposite, it provides the opportunity for fun for you and your team! And remember, sometimes it's the little things that make the big-gest difference. Here's an example:

I have offices in both London and Chicago. Prior to one of my visits, Sarah Rucinski in our Chicago office had gone above and beyond in her preparation for my busy two weeks of meetings. So before leaving the UK, I asked her if there was a 'British' gift I could bring with me to show my appreciation.

Her response was simple — some English tea, crumpets, and a jar of marmalade. Easy, I thought, until she added another item to her list — an English prince! I like a fun challenge, and so, in Chief Engagement Officer mode (and with help from my incredible assistant, Jayne), I came up with a solution.

A few days later I walked into my Chicago office carrying a bag containing tea, crumpets, and marmalade, with my other arm around Prince Harry's shoulders. As I couldn't quite pull off getting a real-life prince to accompany me to Chicago to surprise her, I instead had a life-sized cardboard cut-out of one. Sarah was beside herself. It was fun.

Whilst engagement can be fun, as Chief Engagement Officer you don't need to be the funniest person in the world, the best presenter, or the most outgoing. I've met many owners who aren't these things but who deeply care about their organisations, their people, and how engaged they are. They share their passion for engagement in the way they communicate one on one, in team meetings, and in writing. When it's done with authenticity, everyone in the organisation realises that they are focused on and passionate about engagement in the business — and that in turn helps keep their people focused and passionate.

Don't think that, as an Engaged Owner, you have to have all the answers — you don't. Focus on your strengths and empower your team to focus on theirs. One of our early Engagement Multiplier customers was an entrepreneur who had recently installed a new managing director in his company — quite a substantial enterprise. The new MD had worked within the business for several years and knew it well. When discussing our confidential feedback tools, he said, 'I'm a little worried because I don't think I have all the answers where areas for improvement or concerns are identified.' My response was, 'Of course you're not going to have all the answers — and you're not expected to. As MD and Chief Engagement Officer of the business, it's reasonable to expect you to be very clear on the organisation's purpose and have a vision you're committed to. It's not reasonable to expect you to have all the answers to the challenges that your organisation faces. One of the great things about having an Engaged Organisation is that so many of the answers can be provided from the people within the business, if you empower them to do so. Not only should you allow them to identify areas where focus is required, you should also allow them to have input in solving the problems rather than trying to come up with all the answers yourself.' I continued: 'Over time, providing that you persist in your commitment to engagement, responsibility naturally gets taken up by the people within the business. As that ownership responsibility transfers, the whole Engaged Organisation takes on an energy of its own, causing other people to start suggesting improvements. Focusing on engagement becomes a common language that everyone understands.'

It's worth noting at this point that engagement is a two-way street. When great things happen, Engaged Owners don't lock the door and pop the bubbly. They celebrate success with their teams. When things go wrong, they accept responsibility instead of looking for scapegoats. They look to learn from situations.

Engaged Owners strive to create a culture of open communication that's rich in feedback and recognition. They're also willing to accept feedback from people within the organisation who are able to provide relevant input.

Engaged Owners never say, 'My way or the highway.' They're aware of their strengths, but they're also aware of their limitations. They understand that the only way you build anything of significance is through teamwork, and they understand the value of having feedback from an engaged team.

As the owner of a business, you know when you are authentically focused on the importance of engagement. Does that mean your actions send that message to your team? The best way to find out is to have your organisation complete The Engaged Organisation Scorecard. The score will show very clearly how your organisation perceives you in terms of how engaged you are. Don't be frightened by that. Some of the best results I've seen come from organisations in which the owners get their score, sit down with their teams, acknowledge it, reinforce their commitment to being engaged, and then ask their team for further feedback on things they could do to score higher in the future. They get the most amazing insight from the feedback.

In fact, I've noticed how quickly owners move to engaged status when they use the Scorecard or Engagement Multiplier. The very act of committing to engagement, scoring it, following up, and taking action raises scores.

Engaged Organisations are much easier to own and run than disengaged ones. They have lower employee turnover, lower waste, and best of all, higher morale. As I said at the beginning of this book, it's all about the 'company' you've always dreamt about. If your workplace is where people like to be because the hours fly by, it's a much happier environment for everyone. The last thing you want to do is make Monday morning the low point of the week for yourself and your team! In simple terms, it's not the organisation that motivates and engages its people; *people* motivate people. And as Chief Engagement Officer, it all begins with you.

There's a hard way and there's an easy way to grow a business, and the good news is you have a choice.

The hard way is without engagement. I believe that it's very difficult to fulfil your potential if you don't pursue engagement. Ask yourself, by not focusing on engagement to unlock the potential in your business, are you making life more difficult for yourself than it needs to be?

The easy way to grow you business is to remember, at all times, that you are the Chief Engagement Officer. Let's question each of the components that make up an Engaged Owner. Do you:

- Have a purpose and a vision you're passionate about and that keeps you on a forward trajectory?

- Share your inspiration and motivation and connect your leaders to the purpose and vision?

- Have a written plan for your own future?

- Embrace change and innovation?

- Have genuine concern for your employees, actively encouraging them to fulfil their own potential?

- Lead by example as the Chief Engagement Officer, showing passion for creating an Engaged Organisation?

Let's take a look at these questions and detail how to make them true for you.

### Do you have both a purpose and a vision you're passionate about that keeps you on a forward trajectory?

This is the first thing you need to do!

In the chapter on Engaged Purpose we covered the fundamental importance of this element. A defined purpose allows you to define the 'why'. The vision enables you to state where the business is heading — which I hope is onward, in an upward and exciting direction!

I have an Engaged Purpose for Engagement Multiplier, and I am passionate about it. As I mentioned, my big vision is enabling 100 million people to become measurably more engaged. Can you imagine the impact of *100 million* individuals being more engaged at work? I can! So what's your big vision? Are you personally sold on it? If not, stop right here! You need to get this in place before moving on. Until you're sold on your vision, you can't sell your team on it.

### Do you share your inspiration and motivation and connect your leaders to the purpose and vision?

In my visual representation of an Engaged Organisation, you'll see that the Engaged Owner connects with leaders and employees around the purpose. Obviously, you have to demonstrate your commitment to true engagement to the whole company. Yet, as the Engaged Owner, your first priority is to connect your leaders to the purpose and your vision. Your leaders need to accept the engagement mandates you have set and be capable of implementing them within their teams. This is *key* to engagement success. Leadership is the link between ownership and employees. Don't make it a weak link. Share and discuss your engagement agenda with leadership, and invite them to develop initiatives that will advance it. When they take some ownership in, become personally connected to, and invested in it, they will be able to authentically engage your employees. If your leaders are uninterested or incapable of advancing your engagement agenda, then, as they say at Disney, invite them to find their happiness elsewhere.

A comedian once told me, 'The best way to learn a joke is to tell it to five people.' The same principle applies with engagement. If you share your inspiration and motivation with your leaders and team members on a regular basis, it reinforces it for you and it lifts them up.

## Do you have a written plan for your own future?

To be an Engaged Owner, you have to be engaged with your own personal future. One of the easiest ways to do that is to have a written plan for your time here on Earth.

For over 20 years, I've consulted with successful entrepreneurs. These men and women wouldn't dream of running their business without a business plan or running a project without a project plan. And yet, astonishingly, the only plan they have for themselves is a written plan for when they're dead — a will. I've seen first hand what a huge difference it makes when business owners create a written plan for themselves for whilst they're alive, a plan that's aligned with what they're trying to achieve professionally and in the business world.

If you're going to encourage your employees to create plans for their own engaged futures — something I regard as an important aspect of an Engaged Organisation — you really need to be walking the talk. It doesn't need to be a fifty-page document; it just needs to be what works for you. Many of my clients have pared their written plan for their lives down to one page.

Many years ago, I travelled to the US and listened to a visionary thinker named Jim Rohn. One of the phrases he used was, 'People don't plan to fail; they simply fail to plan.' If you're going to be an Engaged Owner, you must be in control of your life both inside and outside the business. If you don't have a written plan for your future, it's very difficult to be in control of it. For example, the world is littered with business owners who built profitable companies at the expense of personal relationships with people they deeply care about. A written plan helps you focus on the key areas inside and outside your business, with the result that you become a better, more effective, and more Engaged Owner.

Later in this book, I will show you why it's fundamentally important to encourage your team members to have their own written plans and for your organisation to help them achieve their goals and dreams. When you help people to achieve what's important to them, they will help you achieve what's important to you. As Zig Ziglar famously said, 'You can get anything you want by helping enough other people get what *they* want.'

You can't expect your team to do things that you won't do for yourself. And you can't authentically suggest they have a written plan if you don't.

You have to walk the talk.

## Do you embrace change and innovation?

Great owners embrace change. Many things in our world are not the same today as they were even a few short years ago. You probably use Uber instead of taking a taxi. You buy your music online instead of in a record shop. You may text instead of calling. And yet, so many people think that nothing in their *own* industries will ever change, and that they will always be able to do things the same old way.

Engaged Owners know better. They're not just up to speed — they're ahead of the crowd. Steve Jobs didn't do market research before he created the iPod, the iPhone, or the iPad. He just thought about what his market would want and then gave it to them. Likewise, Henry Ford said, 'If I had asked the public what they wanted, they would never have asked for an automobile — they would have just wanted faster horses.'

The prevalence of technology has sped up our world in ways unimaginable not very long ago. The microchip has had as much influence on the world as Gutenberg's invention of movable type. Because of it, it's possible to disseminate information, communicate with others, do deals, and learn what's happening faster than ever before in human history. Engaged Owners embrace this era of head-spinning change instead of shying away from it. As a result, they position themselves to not only benefit from the latest developments in technology and business, but also to actually create them.

### Do you feel genuinely concerned about your employees, actively encouraging them to fulfil their own potential?

Engaged Owners are genuinely concerned about their employees. If you employ millennials, you probably know that the best way to keep them is to train them, at your expense, for their next position with their next employer! Today, younger employees bring to the workplace an expectation that they will not simply be asked to perform their jobs, but to learn new ones. They are happiest and most satisfied when they are not just working, but growing. You need to recognise that employees today feel entitled to personal growth, and you need to do what it takes to meet this vital expectation. If good employees aren't growing, they'll leave for a place where they *can* grow. So it's not enough for you alone to stay inspired and motivated; you need to grow and embrace change. You must provide inspiration, motivation, and opportunities for everyone on your team. Otherwise, they'll take the lift to ground level one day and you'll never see them again.

Even when you get it right, many will leave anyway. But it will be a good thing. Let me explain why.

Many years ago, my personal assistant at the time, Anna, shared with me that one of her goals was to spend some time living and working in New York. As I had no plans to open a business in New York, we worked together to enable her goal to be a reality.

That meant that I ended up having to replace Anna because she left. But do you think for the time she worked with me she was engaged? Do you think she helped me both find and train her replacement? Absolutely! When you have Engaged Employees whom you help to achieve their goals, business becomes so much easier. Most of the time, if an employee's goals and dreams are really important to them, they're going to pursue them anyway, with or without your help. If you do help them, you'll be in greater control of the situation and have transparency about what's going to happen, which will allow you to run your business more effectively.

There is a fabulous restaurant and boutique hotel near Oxford. It's called Belmond Le Manoir aux Quat'Saisons. It's my favourite restaurant in the world. Its founder, Raymond Blanc, is a visionary with a purpose, and he's one of the best examples of an Engaged Owner I know. A true standard bearer, Le Manoir is renowned for incredible service, food, atmosphere, and hospitality. If you haven't been, it's worth putting on your written plan!

So why do I mention this here? Well, if you're fortunate enough to go, politely ask for a 'backstage' tour (and tell them I recommended it). Incredibly engaged employees will proudly show you behind the scenes. You'll experience the passion and personal growth that the team enjoys. Le Manoir takes great pleasure in delivering what is regarded as some of the finest training and skill development in its business sector. If you want to pursue a career in hospitality, having Le Manoir on your resume is big news. When it comes to people development, Le Manoir actively encourages people to spread their wings, taking their well-honed skills to other restaurants and hotels all over the world. Le Manoir takes its responsibility for training other businesses' staff very seriously. They love upholding standards. They think of themselves almost as a training academy. To most business owners, this would feel like a crazy way to run a company. Train people so they leave? But it works. Really, really well.

And a number of the talented staff fall in love with the place and don't want to leave. Their authentic passion is palpable. As we travel, my wife and I frequently meet former Le Manoir staff members in similar high-end establishments in other countries. I've not heard one former employee have anything but good words to say. Le Manoir finds it easier to recruit than many of its competitors. People want to work there.

It's an Engaged Organisation that provides growth opportunities for its team members so they can fulfil their potential.

And the food and hospitality are second to none.

I love it.

Now, do I sound like an Engaged Customer?

As they say at Disney, 'It's expensive to train employees who leave. But it's even more expensive not to train employees who stick around!'

### Do you lead by example as the Chief Engagement Officer, showing passion for creating an Engaged Organisation?

Another way to spot Engaged Owners is by their willingness to engage leaders and team members to create an engaged culture. The era of the aloof, distant executive who is nothing more than a photo in an annual report or a talking head in an occasional cross-enterprise town hall meeting is a thing of the past. Engaged Owners not only manage by walking around, they manage by connecting with their leaders and team members in a deep and meaningful way. There are few Lone Rangers at the top of the business world! The most successful businesses are ones in which the boss has his ear to the ground because he spends as much time at ground level as he does in the penthouse. An Engaged Owner could be thought of (if this image is not too paternalistic for you) as the head of a family who still makes time for family dinners. The TV isn't on, no one's texting, and there is actual face-to-face communication. Can you say this about your business? Or for that matter, your family?

An Engaged Owner celebrates his success with his team, creating an open culture of communication rich in feedback and recognition. That's a long way of saying that if you don't share the credit, the people who created success for you will go create it for someone else. If there's bad news, do people in your organisation feel empowered to bring it to you? Or does your business embrace the unfortunate attitude of 'shoot the messenger'? Too often, owners talk about 'open communication', but what they really mean is, 'Only bring me good news!' How open are you to hearing the truth, as uncomfortable as it may be? The easiest way to resolve a crisis is to keep it from happening in the first place. That can only happen when open communication enables leaders and the owner himself (or herself) to know what's really going on. Is there an early-warning system fostered by open communication in your enterprise? Or are you just crossing your fingers and hoping that everything's going to be okay? The highway of business is littered with the wreckage of companies that simply closed their eyes and hoped for the best.

## GOLDEN RULES / HINTS AND TIPS

*The goal is progress, not perfection.* If, as Chief Engagement Officer, you follow my model of simply measuring engagement every ninety days, you will be presented with so many opportunities to take action. Play a game you can win. You're not going to be able to do everything at once — perfection rarely happens. But if you just took three key actions a quarter, that's twelve a year, and over a five-year period, that's sixty actions taken to improve engagement. Can you imagine what your business would look like with sixty engagement initiatives completed? In order for you to successfully create an engaged team, they need to see that there's action being taken on an ongoing basis and that it's not just the latest fad.

***Tell the truth!*** There's always danger in attempting to put a happy face on every work situation, especially when things get difficult and painful. Your people appreciate the truth, and you can bet your team is more aware of what's going on than you realise. So be clear and straightforward when dealing with troublesome issues. This builds trust, and trust builds engagement. Integrity is a key attribute of an effective Engaged Owner.

When we speak to our clients at Engagement Multiplier, we say there's no such thing as a bad score. The score is the score. In fact, it will be disengaging if you don't tell the truth. If there are problems, face up to them. Fears, when faced, disappear.

***Strive to create a progress culture, not a perfection culture.*** People have to be allowed to try and fail. They must also be encouraged to move projects forward even though every single piece of the puzzle isn't yet in place. Your ultimate goal as the Engaged Owner should be to build a self-managing company. How does that happen? When you give leadership and employees a good measure of autonomy and a firm framework for what needs to be done and by when, you empower real engagement.

Too many companies pretend that they allow their people to try things and fail. In reality, office politics takes over and failure isn't something to be celebrated — it's an opportunity to get rid of someone who stands in the way of some opportunistic individual's path to the top. This is no way to run a railroad! I'm not suggesting that you allow resources — time, money, people, or all three — to be committed willy-nilly to any project that strikes someone's fancy. There have to be boundaries in place. But the real question is whether you are willing to make a commitment to let people try and fail.

The great motivator Tony Robbins speaks of redefining words so that what we say becomes more effective and useful. Most people, he says, define the term *success* far too narrowly. In his mind, success means 'taking chances, some of which work out and some of which don't'. If you can accept that definition of success, then the term *failure* can be erased from your enterprise's entire lexicon!

*Recognise and celebrate.* When individuals demonstrate outstanding initiative in achieving company goals or improving engagement, don't just make a note of such things — reward those people. Give out company prizes and meaningful recognition to motivate everyone to fully engage in the pursuit of excellence.

---

### Engaged Organisation Action: How Did You Score?

If you're using the Engagement Multiplier Program, you will have already seen how you've scored and the direction you should be taking to improve your score further.

If you're using the book or downloaded Scorecard, go to EngagementMultiplier.com/en-gb/eobook for advice and guidance on actions you can consider taking to improve your score.

---

As a Chief Engagement Officer, armed with an Engaged Purpose and clarity on what it takes to be an Engaged Owner, you should now understand the areas where you need to focus. I am sure that you already do many of the things I've mentioned in this chapter — but there may be other things you will now do slightly differently or new approaches you will now take. My advice to you is, don't try to do everything at once, but do take action.

In the next chapter, we'll talk about how you can transfer your passion for your purpose and vision and connect the next important group in the organisation, Engaged Leaders.

Chapter 6

# Engaged Leaders

*Empowering your growth integrators*

*'You manage things; you lead people.'*
—Rear Admiral Grace Murray Hopper—

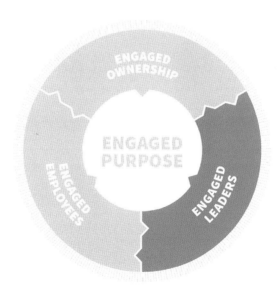

Engaged Leaders are, in simple terms, growth integrators. They're
the people who provide the critical link between aspiration and

achievement, between your organisation's Engaged Purpose and vision, and between purpose and motivation of your team to make all this a reality.

In the last chapter, I explained that most organisations *can* function with a small number of employees who are less engaged than the others. However, when disengagement creeps up to leadership, the cost (financial and otherwise) is substantial. There's plenty of evidence supporting that. Gallup's recent *State of The American Manager* survey reveals some shocking statistics:

- Managers account for at least seventy percent of the variance in employee engagement scores across business units.

- Only thirty-five percent of managers are engaged, whilst fifty-one percent are not engaged and fourteen percent are actively disengaged.

- Managers' engagement has a direct impact on employees' engagement. Employees who are supervised by highly engaged managers are fifty-nine percent more likely to be engaged than those supervised by actively disengaged managers.

- At some point in their career, one in two employees has left a job to get away from his or her manager.

- Gallup estimates that 'disengaged' managers cost the US economy alone $77 billion to $96 billion annually through their impact on those they manage. And when we factor in the impact of 'actively disengaged' managers, those figures jump to $319 billion to $398 billion annually.

- Whilst great managers consistently engage their teams

to achieve outstanding performance, bad managers cost businesses billions of dollars each year, and having too many of them can bring down a company.

Gallup goes on to say, 'Until organisations can increase their percentage of engaged managers, they have little hope of increasing their percentage of engaged employees. The cascade effect essentially means that employees' engagement is directly influenced by their managers' engagement.' In a nutshell, disengaged managers create disengaged employees. Ask yourself, how many people have you employed who turned up on day one with the intention of switching off? None, I bet. Otherwise, you wouldn't have recruited them in the first place!

Gallup uses the term *managers*. For me, though, creating engagement takes leadership — not just from you but from key team members within your organisation. One of the key differentiators between a leader and manager is that a leader, through their actions, inspires and motivates others. A manager, on the other hand, is someone who might be very organised and effective at getting things done but doesn't engender the same level of loyalty or devotion as a leader. That's not to say that managers aren't incredibly valuable and highly regarded, but as the quote at the top of this chapter tells us, 'You manage things; you lead people.'

Engaged leadership is all about having leaders who demonstrate a commitment to inspire and connect team members to your Engaged Purpose on a continuous basis — and this is fundamental to creating an Engaged Organisation. It creates a culture in which every member of the team is encouraged to put his or her own stamp on the organisation — innovate and driving improvement within the context of a common vision and purpose for your organisation that your leaders keep front of mind.

Engaged Leaders motivate their team members to do their best in two ways: First, they view their people as *people*. This may seem like a very obvious point — of course people are people! Yet, too many employers only see their employees in terms of their job descriptions, not in terms of their humanity. Hotel housekeepers aren't just the number of rooms they can clean in a week. They may be smarter than a lot of the people higher up in the organisation, and yet they're often a lot closer to the guests than the executives who run the company. So an Engaged Leader looks at such individuals with respect and dignity instead of measuring them by how much (or how little) they are paid per hour.

A great leader doesn't assume they know what's important to their team members — they ask. When they ask, they listen. When they've listened, they provide feedback. When they've provided feedback, they take action. A great example comes, yet again, from Disney. A housekeeper told her supervisor that the hardest part of her job was moving her heavy cart from one room to the next. Would it be possible to mechanise the carts? Disney studied the matter and quickly concluded that motorising the carts would increase the housekeepers' productivity so much that the carts would pay for themselves. As a result, Disney motorised not just all the housekeeper carts in its hotel properties across the planet, but also the food, drink, and souvenir carts in its theme parks worldwide. The cost savings were enormous, all because the company's culture took seriously the thoughts of all its 'cast members' — including the housekeepers.

Another Disney housekeeper started creating 'towel animals' for guests in their hotel rooms. Now, every Disney guest, whether in a hotel or on a Disney cruise, can expect to find towel animals after a day of 'exhausting' fun. Did a highly paid consultant or executive come up with these innovations? No, a housekeeper did.

The second way in which Engaged Leaders inspire their team members is by setting a standard for excellence themselves — and just like you, the owner, they need to walk the talk. They, too, need to be engaged with their own future and, importantly, with your organisation's purpose.

If they're not engaged, their team members will see straight through them. It's simply not reasonable for an organisation to expect employees to give any attention to engagement if the people who own and lead the business aren't demonstrably committed to it themselves.

So what stops a leader from being engaged? What are the barriers? It could be that they don't truly appreciate the power of engagement — they don't know what they don't know. They may have tried different programs in the past that haven't had the desired effect, and so they're dubious. They might think that engagement means more work for them, and as a result only pay lip service to it. Perhaps they're concerned about opening themselves up to their teams — especially if they ever need to make difficult decisions or provide feedback on poor performance. They may feel vulnerable about receiving feedback on their own leadership qualities. Or it could be that they're just used to doing things a certain way and don't want to rock the boat. Many of these concerns are understandable, but none are insurmountable.

On the flip side, what are the signs that your leaders *are* engaged? Ask yourself the following: Do they focus on engagement at an organisational and local level, coaching and mentoring their teams from the trenches instead of ivory towers? Do they develop and hire great people, then get out of the way, helping these people become great leaders themselves? Do they put their teams (and not themselves) first and expect (and receive) the best from their people and not the worst? Are they their teams' greatest ambassadors, leading them to achieve great results?

A word of warning here. Just because a division (for example) is getting results, it doesn't automatically mean it's engaged. It's possible that the head of that division could still be a disengaged leader. When this happens, there can be a tendency for owners to say, 'I'd better not rock the boat. It's working. That division is making profit, and I'll leave it be.' But think of it this way: If that division is achieving results with a disengaged leader, what would be possible with an *engaged* leader? The decision for you to make as an Engaged Owner is whether the pain of change, of taking a disengaged leader and helping them to become engaged, is worth the reward.

Let's look more closely at each of the key components of an Engaged Leader:

- They are passionate about your organisation's Engaged Purpose.

- They break down barriers.

- They put people first, show appreciation, and encourage a culture of self-improvement.

- They feel connected to Engaged Owners and empowered to proactively translate purpose into action.

- They create effective, regular communication and feedback with team members and conduct open, two-way reviews on a least a quarterly basis.

Let's expand on each in turn.

**Engaged Leaders are passionate about the organisation's goals, developing and expanding their own powerful 'engaged futures', whilst integrating the goals of the business owners with those of the other team members.**

As the owner, you are responsible for curating vision and purpose and sharing that with leaders in such a way that they connect with it. Leaders typically have different departments, different areas of responsibility, and make different contributions to the organisation. An Engaged Leader is able to connect the dots and understands the contribution they can make to help achieve the organisation's goals. In turn, they are able to connect their team members to the vision, purpose, and goals and, wherever possible, create alignment between the team members' goals and those of the business. Done well, this is very powerful.

**Engaged Leaders also break down barriers, putting people first by getting to know them, showing appreciation, and encouraging a culture of self-improvement.**

People want more from a workplace than just work. We've witnessed an unfortunate diminution in the importance of community activities in Western society over the last few years. Everything from religious institutions to volunteer activities, has suffered from the time crunch brought on by increasing work pressures and the advent of personal technology devices. People spend more time either working or on Facebook than face-to-face with loved ones or people in their neighbourhoods. In many communities in the US and the UK, people don't even know their neighbour, something unimaginable in past years.

As a result, many people look to the workplace to provide social contact, meaning, and direction in their lives. They're looking for much more than a pay cheque. The Engaged Leader recognises this and seeks to provide those qualities and experiences in order to create that vital sense of meaning in people's lives. In just the same way that an Engaged Organisation is the 'company' you dream about, for your Leaders and employees it's also the 'company' they dream about.

Engaged Leaders have a far stronger emotional connection with the people who work with and for them. Why? Because they're invested in them as people rather than just as workers. If leaders don't care about their team members, then those leaders can't really expect their team members to care about what they're trying to achieve. Demonstrating a lack of care forces the leader-employee relationship to be purely transactional — an employee exchanges time for money. We already know from previous chapters that money is not the main reason people go to work.

When leaders create an emotional connection and are invested in their people instead of just thinking of them as a resource, the dynamic moves to a different level — and so does their loyalty, commitment, and yes, engagement. It's not about just walking through the workplace handing out chocolate; it's about getting to know the people holistically — as grown-up humans with their own objectives and goals.

Ask yourself, are all the leaders in your organisation as interested in what they can do for their workers as much as what the business can do for them (your leaders)? It's a really interesting test.

If you've ever taken a yoga class, you know that the last word the teacher utters is the Sanskrit word *namaste*, accompanied by a small bow. The word roughly translates thus: 'The divinity in me salutes the divinity in you.' Is this how your Engaged Leaders view your team members? I hope so! (And so do they!)

### Feel connected to Engaged Owners and empowered to proactively translate purpose into action.

Engaged Leaders don't only create great relationships with their employees. They also feel connected to the owner and empowered to proactively translate the purpose and vision into action. If this is to happen, of course, it's up to you to help make it happen. How much time do you afford your leaders? Do they have the same relationship with you that we advocate they have with their team members? They have their own human needs, too; they need to feel fulfilled in the workplace. Are you conscious of those needs, and are you attempting to meet them? Remember, engagement starts at the top — with you.

When leaders are asked what motivates them, it's often autonomy: the freedom to carry out their work, make decisions, and deliver results in a way they think is right. It's about being trusted and being given space to just get on with the job that motivates them.

When they're doing so using the wonderful framework and context of your Engaged Purpose, it's a win-win.

**Effective, regular communication and feedback with team members, including open, two-way reviews on at least a quarterly basis.**

Communication is critical to the success of an Engaged Organisation. It is, by far, the most common thing mentioned in Engagement Multiplier's clients' team feedback. Employees at all levels want to know what's going on. Leaders who truly communicate and connect their team with what's happening enjoy loyalty and committed team members. Conversely, those who treat employees like mushrooms (leave them in the dark and feed them dung) unsurprisingly find their 'leadership' role stressful and challenging, as they introduce more problems to solve. Regular communication is essential. Not sure what the team wants to know? Ask them!

Regular, open, two-way reviews are also very important. One of the things I find astonishing is that so many organisations don't complete reviews with team members at all. For those who do, it's often a once-a-year-exercise in which the leader and employee both feel that they're just going through the motions. It's often regarded as somewhat of a waste of time, because it achieves little in the way of tangible results. That's partly because of the time that elapses from one review to the next. And it's a shame — such an unnecessary waste of an opportunity for leaders to truly connect with their team members away from the hustle and bustle of the shop floor.

In an Engaged Organisation, reviews — both formal and informal — take place on an ongoing basis. There's a culture of feedback, celebration of successes, and acknowledgement of contribution on a daily and weekly basis. Reviews are often conducted quarterly and, as a result, become more of a checkpoint: an opportunity to connect with an individual team member on where they're heading in the context of the business's objectives, and what they want to achieve personally. Reviews are a way of making sure that the actions being taken by the employee and by the business are aligned.

Reviews are both backward and forward looking. In an Engaged Organisation, leaders and employees alike treat them as an opportunity to spend some time focused on the individual team member, helping them to understand, with context, their contribution to the wider organisation. The meetings are an opportunity to celebrate what's working and talk about areas where improvements can be made in a way that's both constructive and energising. That they're conducted regularly means they don't block momentum. There's also the opportunity for quick corrective action when required.

Leaders who do all of the above and show they genuinely care will earn the loyalty of the people they lead. The employees, in return, will be willing to discuss their personal goals and how they can align what they're personally trying to achieve with what the business is trying to achieve. You can't, however, expect every leader to jump straight to this point. There's a progression: Communicate, acknowledge, be interested, appreciate the whole person, connect around things they're doing that aren't related to work, and offer support.

Some business owners dismiss this as just window dressing that doesn't support the bottom line. I hope by now I've convinced you that such thinking is self-defeating!

## GOLDEN RULES / HINTS AND TIPS

*Approval and appreciation.* The first step in making sure that a team is as engaged as possible is to demonstrate that leadership approves of and appreciates their work for the company. This is one of the Engaged Leader's key roles. A successful Engaged Leader has to look beyond discontent and focus on the dedication of the team members to the company. When they do, they can find key ways to leverage those team members' qualities to improve their own performances. Engaged Leaders are on the lookout for opportunities to acknowledge the contributions made by the people on their teams in a way that's not false or fabricated, but authentic.

***Put the person ahead of the job.*** The old saying goes that there's no 'I' in *team*. (Although as Michael Jordan pointed out, there is an 'I' in *win!*) When everyone's pulling together to polish off a project, yes, they have to work together to succeed. But ultimately, an engaged team is actually made up of *individuals* who want to be thought of as distinct personalities. Nobody wants to be considered just another part of the herd. This means that Engaged Leaders must spend time getting to know their team members as people and getting in touch with their talents, ambitions, and quirks. This personal touch is essential to engagement at this level.

***Remove the politics.*** Nothing sabotages engagement like the belief that 'the game is rigged'. I'm talking about what should be a very dirty word to any Engaged Leader — politics. Leadership roles within a team should be assigned according to talent, interest, and results, and not for reasons that are unrelated to performance on the job. Complete fairness in organisational matters may sometimes be impossible, but it is a goal that Engaged Leaders should always pursue.

***Break down barriers.*** Whenever they can, Engaged Leaders should encourage workers to connect not only with others in their own departments, but also with people in other departments. This kind of cross-pollination frequently eliminates tunnel vision and allows for some heady brainstorming. For example, someone in production might collaborate with someone in accounting to devise a new, cost-effective way to track supply expenses.

One of the biggest problems in the book publishing industry (as in most industries) is the tendency for departments within the company to become siloed and fail to communicate with other departments. At some of the best-known book-publishing firms, the editors who acquire books have little contact with the marketing division and only see the sales force three times a year. It's hard to make a business succeed when the key people have no idea what happens to their work after they throw it 'over the wall'. Is this true in your business?

*Be passionate about your job* **and** *about the company's goals.* If leadership isn't excited about what it's doing, or about achieving important organisational goals, the team won't be, either. Team members take their cues from leadership. When an Engaged Leader takes care to convey the spirit of any endeavour, it adds energy and excitement to everybody's effort. How are your leaders conveying their enthusiasm for your company's goals? Are they communicating them clearly, effectively, and repeatedly, or are they keeping their cards too close to their chests?

*Open up to their team.* Engaged Leaders need to be prepared to open up a bit to the people who work for them. If they're entirely private, isolated, and clinical about the work they do — not showing their own humanity or what they find exciting in their own lives — don't expect their team members to share with them personally in return. If they're closed off as leaders and purely focused on what's going on in the business, they'll never be Engaged Leaders, because their people won't open up to them.

I'm not for one minute suggesting your leaders should share intimate details of their private lives — that may be inappropriate. What I *am* suggesting is, there are things that excite them outside of their work. It's good for them to give their team members a glimpse of these things — and they may even find some common ground in areas they didn't realise.

---

### Engaged Organisation Action: How Did You Score?

If you're using the Engagement Multiplier Program, you will have already seen how you've scored and the direction you should be taking to improve your score further.

If you're using the book or downloaded Scorecard, go to EngagementMultiplier.com/en-gb/eobook for advice and guidance on actions you can consider taking to improve your score.

---

As an Engaged Owner, you appreciate the importance of having a leadership team that is engaged. It makes achieving the business's vision goals and purpose so much easier. It enables you as the owner to focus on the purpose and vision, whilst creating an organisation that can become self-managing (whilst still growing!) if you want it to. You cannot create an Engaged Organisation without Engaged Leaders.

In the next chapter we are going to look at the final element of the Engaged Organisation — Engaged Employees. This is where engagement meets the outside world.

# Chapter 7

# Engaged Employees

*Your front line: Where engagement
meets the outside world*

*'The way your employees feel is the way your customers will feel.'*
—Sybil F. Stershic—

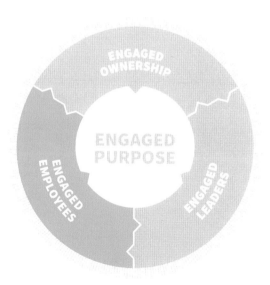

ngaging your employees is about unlocking their potential so that, in turn, they help you unlock yours — and that of your organisation. It's about engaging their hearts and minds to enable them to be the best they can be, developing your organisation's relationship with them in a way that turns good employees into great people. I love this quote from Betty Bender: 'When people come to work, they shouldn't have to leave their hearts at home.'

I couldn't agree more.

When an employee is truly engaged they become more animated, creative, and positive. They transfer the 'electricity' I referred to in previous chapters to everyone who comes into contact with your business — and in doing so, your employees become your greatest brand ambassadors. Engaged Employees create Engaged Customers and, let's face it, that's what we all want. It's been said many times before that it's not people's actions you remember, it's the way those actions made you feel. If you think back to one of your own incredible customer experiences, chances are you'll remember the Engaged Employee who was responsible. Likewise, you probably remember when you last dealt with a disengaged employee.

Employees are the people in your organisation who sit at the front line — where engagement meets the outside world — but until you've set the foundations I've explained in the previous three chapters, it's premature to expect your employees to be engaged at any meaningful level. The traditional approach to creating engagement has been to start with employees and customers, but starting with employees is problematic and rarely delivers the results you're looking for. Instead, you need to begin by investing the owners and leaders in the Engaged Purpose. Long gone are the days when employees blindly subscribed to the mantra 'Do as I say, not as I do.' For the best employees, today's world is full of opportunity, and they know it. A better motto for the twenty-first century is: 'Help them achieve and they won't want to leave.'

I've met many business owners who, for myriad reasons, don't truly understand the untapped goldmine of resource and growth potential their employees represent. And even if they do, they don't know how to unlock it. They often don't look beyond their leadership for ideas for improvements, savings and innovations. That's a shame, because their employees have much to offer. Time and time again, I've seen business owners break into huge smiles when they see the (anonymous, and therefore honest) feedback their teams provide through the Engagement Multiplier program. There are almost always common themes in the employee feedback. Our experience has shown that some of simplest suggestions can have the most profound effect on individual and organisational engagement levels. The amazing thing about these suggestions is that they're rarely about what the employee can get out of the organisation (more pay or holiday allowance, for example) and more about what they want to put in.

Employees are proud, excited, and thankful to be given a voice. It's fair to say that some feedback is critical (although ninety-nine percent of the time it's constructive) — but much of it is positive, and sometimes genuinely surprising and heartwarming. Here's an outstanding example of an anonymous and confidential piece of feedback from an employee of an Engaged Organisation utilising the Engagement Multiplier program:

*'I love this company immensely and I know that sometimes my goals as a customer advocate are the opposite to what makes good business sense. Thank you for always listening and implementing my ideas where applicable and able. It feels great to be respected in that manner and I hope that in the future I can become a more integral part of keeping people believing in the business. This survey asked about future goals and I can tell you most definitely I have one to work to build us to 100,000 members, one renewal at a time. I have never been treated half as well by my employer as I am today. I'm pretty low in the hierarchy here but I am consistently treated like a prince. I hope with my very deepest heart of hearts that this is the last place I ever work. Thank you so much.'*

Now that's an Engaged Employee! Wouldn't you just love an organisation full of people with that type of enthusiasm and commitment?

## Two Types of Engagement

The first type is transactional: In other words, reward people for the role they play. Employees deserve to be compensated fairly. You can't ignore the fact that they're giving you twenty, thirty, forty, or more hours of their lives each week. But survey after survey shows that financial reward usually ranks fourth, fifth, or even lower on the pecking order of what employees say engages them. If employees only feel a connection to your business at a transactional level, you have a problem. As Simon Sinek says: 'When people are financially invested, they want a return. When people are emotionally invested, they want to contribute.'

To truly succeed in the engagement world, you and your leaders need to appreciate the second type of engagement: emotional engagement. Emotional engagement means that work becomes more than just a job, that an employee is just as motivated by what they can do for you and your organisation (and you) as they are about what it can do for them. Emotional engagement is about appreciation, respect, acknowledgment, support, understanding, and being valued. Addressing the emotional aspects of engagement doesn't require complex management or leadership training; it just requires common sense and a basic understanding of how to treat people as people with consideration and respect. After all, your employees are human beings, not merely human 'resources' or human 'capital'.

I started this book by saying: 'Engagement is magical. More specifically, the outcomes delivered by engagement are magical.' When you successfully engage your employees, the impact is magnified and your persistence rewarded handsomely. The magical outcomes I refer to will be enjoyed not only by you, but by your leaders, employees, and customers.

Engagement breeds engagement.

Engaged Employees are inspired by the organisation's Engaged Purpose, Owners, and Leaders. They use their progress in the workplace as a foundation for greater personal futures. They understand how their role contributes to the organisation's success, often suggesting improvements to enhance both their own and the business's performance. They enjoy trusting and open communication with their leaders and bring their 'whole selves' to work.

Some structure is helpful, however, to achieve the best levels of engagement. I've said for many years that we often do our best work when we have structure and framework, but the flexibility to operate with freedom within it.

All the structure you need has already been shared in this book: Develop an Engaged Purpose, Engaged Ownership, and Engaged Leadership; create a way to consistently and predictably measure how the business and the various elements are doing; and provide every team member with a voice so they can be a part of creating The Engaged Organisation.

By analysing the many thousands of employee feedback points provided through the Engagement Multiplier program, I've developed a simple twelve-point structure for what engages employees:

### 'Connect them to "why" and they will aim high'

As I said in the chapter 'Engaged Purpose', you need a purpose that connects with your front-line people. It gives them a 'why', makes them proud to come to work, and provides context for everything they do. The idea of people holding on to a job just for security and working for one organisation for their entire lives is largely a thing of the past. For the most part, people inherently want to invest more than just their time in the business they work for. But to sustain that desire, they need to feel a connection to what the business stands for and why, so that what they do has meaning.

### 'Lead by your action, and you will get traction'

For all the reasons I've already shared in previous chapters, employees need to believe and see the owners' and leaders' ongoing commitment to engagement. There's a saying I heard some time ago: 'If you want to fly with eagles, don't hang out with turkeys.' Now, I'm not for one minute suggesting that any member of your team is a turkey(!), but as I mentioned above, it's unreasonable to try to raise employee engagement levels if owners and leaders aren't leading from the front. In other words, *they* need to be eagles!

### 'Clarity on their role to support the business as a whole'

For every role in your organisation, it's crucial that there's a position statement clearly articulating what the role is, why it's important, and how it fits with your Engaged Purpose. The difference in performance between employees who understand their role and how it fits into an organisation's purpose and those who don't is like night and day. Why? Because one has context and clarity and the other is just doing the job. There's the old story about a man who passed by three men digging a ditch. He asked each what he was doing.

The first man said, 'I'm digging a ditch — what does it look like?'

The second man said, 'I'm making twelve bucks an hour.'

The third man said, 'I'm building a cathedral.'

I think the meaning is clear.

### 'When they're clear on the goal, they'll achieve in the role'

Having clear deliverables is not about how to do something. That's what training is for. It's about providing a framework for what needs to be delivered by when. Dan Sullivan has created a wonderful tool called The Impact Filter®, which provides a simple structure for defining the purpose (in this context of the role), the objective and what needs to be delivered for there be to a successful outcome. Over the years, I've completed hundreds of Impact Filters for both roles and projects. My experience has been that if you clearly define the end result you're look-ing to achieve, then Engaged Employees will ask for help if they need it and, more often than not, they will simply get on with the task at hand — with the full knowledge of what the desired outcome is — and deliver it.

**'An open feedback line means they're motivated to shine'**
As I touched on earlier, for feedback to be genuinely valuable to the employee and the organisation, it needs to take two forms: (1) regular, structured, two-way feedback and (2) ongoing, informal feedback.

- *Regular, structured, two-way feedback:* By this I mean scheduled review meetings on at least a quarterly basis (as described in the last chapter). By keeping these sessions simple but effective, they provide the perfect opportunity to treat the employee as an individual, not just a cog in the wheel. They're an opportunity for both parties to share success stories, make improvements, and help the employee focus on their strengths instead of pointing out their weaknesses. At the same time, failings can be addressed in a constructive way. The meetings become a touchpoint; employees know their leaders consider them important, therefore so do they. Gone is the apathy that many employees experience when they feel that their review is conducted merely to tick a box on their leader's to-do list.

- *Ongoing, informal, feedback:* This can take many forms — a simple 'how's it going' or a chat over a coffee, for example. Creating an open culture rich in feedback means that when people make progress, they are congratulated, supported and thanked. At the same time they can be given guidance on an ongoing basis to help them achieve deliverables for the role. And you can take this a step further. In my own businesses, I operate a system of 'coachable moments' in which everyone, regardless of position or tenure, feels free to offer words of wisdom, feedback, or advice to anyone in the organisation. The only rule is that it needs to be done with positive intent. And whilst, as a business owner, I've given my team some coachable moments, I can assure you I've received a quite few, too! When people are willing to do this, it's a clear sign they care.

### 'Consistently share, and they'll continue to care'

Humans are innately curious. Your employees not only want to feel connected to the progress they're making personally, they also want to feel connected to how the business as a whole is doing. If they're engaged, they're genuinely interested, they care, and the right communication helps them to perform in their roles more effectively. Company communication can take many forms — emails, intranet updates, or webinars — but what employees love more than anything is to hear the news from the horse's mouth. By hearing owners and leaders speak with passion about the organisation, how well it's doing (or not doing), what the next steps are, and how they can help, employees can to rise to the challenge and put their true engagement into action.

### 'With the resource they require, they continuously aspire'

This may seem obvious, but having the appropriate tools to do the job is important to employees. If an analyst is being asked to provide intelligent feedback on a long list of data and they have a computer that keeps crashing, it will test their patience. If it happens over a prolonged period of time, it will dilute their enthusiasm and ultimately their engagement levels. Your employee doesn't necessarily want the latest gadget or most expensive piece of equipment; they just want something that works and doesn't stand in the way of their doing a great job. Similarly, it's just as important for employees to feel able to draw on resources from else-where in the business to help them out if they're stuck on a problem or need some advice.

### 'When connected as a tribe, as a team they will thrive'

People love the idea of being part of a business family, getting to know each other outside of the roles they play each day in the workplace. At Engagement Multiplier, we actively encourage team get-togethers and social events, activities that help to nurture a community feeling. If the team is doing things together that have nothing to do with work, and bonds are being created that extend beyond their professional lives, this only enhances their ability to thrive as a team. We regularly see feed-back from employees using the Engagement Multiplier program that support this.

Almost every survey I see includes comments from team members about how much they enjoy company socials both within their imme-diate teams and beyond — and how they'd like more of them. This isn't about lavish parties or hiring expensive team-building consultants; it can be something as simple as a drink after work or a bite to eat at lunchtime. I've hosted many team events at my own home, giving the opportunity for families — both work and personal — to come together. Just as having an Engaged Organisation is the company that you've always dreamt about, it's the company they've always dreamt about, too.

### 'Help them to grow, and they won't want to go'

It's highly likely that your organisation includes some team members who are more passionate about engagement than others are. These people are sincerely and actively interested in your organisation's development alongside their own. However, it's also highly likely that you don't have formal leadership positions available for each of them. This is how, at Strategic Coach, something called the 'LEO' role came to be.

LEO stands for 'Leader of an Engaged Organisation', and appropriately, it's something Strategic Coach team members initiated. What's fabulous about this idea is that it allows interested participants to pursue engagement initiatives whilst developing themselves for future formal leadership positions. As of the writing of this book, more than twenty percent of Coach team members have taken up a LEO role.

Can you imagine the power of having twenty percent of your staff voluntarily taking up LEO roles? As I mentioned, your organisation almost certainly has a number of these 'leaders in waiting' already — now, you don't have to keep them waiting any longer. The LEO role provides them with the opportunity to demonstrate leadership in a way that's harmonious with your organisation and its goals. Meanwhile, by allowing them to take ownership of one or more initiatives to improve engagement in your business, you are creating the ultimate Engaged Employees.

And incidentally, there was no carrot-dangling, extra money, or perks attached to the role at Strategic Coach — just support from leaders and owners and, obviously, the ability to make a difference. This gave team members the opportunity to be recognised and perhaps see success reflected in their treatment in future reviews. This approach is a great way to give engagement more profile and energy in your business, and it's worthy of serious consideration.

Following a more traditional path, many business owners make it a point to invest in their employees' continuing education, and I couldn't encourage this more wholeheartedly. Unfortunately, though, I've also seen many business owners make the mistake of spending thousands of dollars on their own development and then baulk at spending a few hundred dollars to develop their employees' capabilities. These owners are missing the key concept here — *invest* — because that investment pays off when the employees bring those new skills back into the workplace. You have to empower your engaged team members to develop their strengths; this will benefit your organisation as much as it benefits them. Most employees crave the opportunity to learn new skills to both enhance the role they perform today and be able to grasp new opportunities.

The Engagement Multiplier Onboarding Team is a terrific example of this. Jocelyn, Taylor, Ashleigh, and Elizabeth have all demonstrated great skill in helping our clients roll out the program to their businesses. The team loves what they do and, at the same time, as Engaged Employees, they have an eye on the future and where they want to take their careers. Each member of the team is met with individually. A career path is agreed upon, and key deliverables and training programs are aligned with their longer-term objectives. All appreciate the opportunity — and are they more engaged as a result? Yes, of course!

The other thing I've done for many years is give my team members a personal development budget. The purpose is to provide them with funding to enhance an existing skill or develop a new one. It doesn't have to be work-related. They could use the budget to learn to play a musical instrument or learn martial arts. They could attend classes on public speaking or learn calligraphy. The boundaries are broad, but in case someone thought it would be amusing to develop his beer-drinking skills, release of the budget does require sign-off by an Engaged Leader! It bears repeating: When you help your employees reach their goals, they're more likely to help you reach yours.

### 'When reward is fair, motivation they'll share'

Reward for me is twofold — financial and non-financial. Whilst money and benefits are rarely the main motivation for an employee to turn up to work for you every day, they do need to feel they're being rewarded fairly — and then it doesn't become an issue. It's also worth remembering that for people to derive value from most employee-benefit packages they have to retire, fall sick, or die! Thus, it's important to include non-financial benefits they can use for reasons not necessarily associated with a negative event nor years in the future. For example, in my own businesses, I introduced flexible working hours, and it was a real game-changer. Many of my employees have families, and they can now pick up the kids from school a few times a week or alter their schedules to do something important for themselves. They manage the system of flexible working responsibly between them to ensure there's no negative impact on the business or our customers — and they do so because they have been given the important gifts of latitude, security, and fairness. Among other things, I also acknowledge, reward, and celebrate every team member's anniversary of joining my businesses, and I do so in a way that's personal to them. For example, one member of my team, Jamie, recently celebrated nine years with my consulting firm. Knowing that he's an avid music fan, I presented him with some iTunes vouchers. Susie, based in the same office, recently celebrated two years with the company — and I walked in with a huge bunch of her favourite flowers. The principle was the same — the reward was personal, and that's what made it rewarding for both them and, selfishly, me. It's great to see the smiles on their faces!

### 'When they're allowed to be free, great results you will see'

I've seen many employees become gradually demoralised by their leaders' micromanagement of them. They see this as a lack of trust in their ability to perform in the role. When a leader feels the need to indiscriminately micromanage, it's often more a reflection of their own shortcomings than those of their employees. One of the questions we ask employees participating in the Engagement Multiplier Program is: What two actions can you take personally, that are not dependent on leadership, to improve engagement?

We ask the question in this exact wording because it guides their responses — specifically, because their suggested actions are not dependent on leadership, they usually don't take much time or money to implement. What's more, if you give them the freedom to bring their own engagement ideas to life, you'll also have the opportunity to share and celebrate successes with them! This is a far more empowering and appealing way to operate instead of you or your leadership team having to sign off on every single piece of detail. Of course, the boundaries need to be clear and sensible so they don't put the business at risk.

### 'Value what they do, and they'll be loyal to you'

Your employees' main focus in life is not to make you rich or more successful, but they'll do that with passion if you help them with what's important to them and show that you appreciate and value their efforts. Remember, employees don't come to a company feeling disengaged — it arises on the job! They have goals and talents, and they want to achieve the former and use the latter. The job of you and your leaders is to see and acknowledge those talents. When you do, you'll find key ways to leverage your employees' qualities to improve their personal performances and your organisation's overall engagement.

Making use of this insight is one of the best ways to show that you *value and appreciate* an employee. When you do this, you build loyalty and motivate the person to do his or her best for you. Of course, depending on the size of the company and the circumstances, this kind of ideal trade-off may not always be possible. But unless you find *personal and meaningful* ways to demonstrate to your employees that you recognise their value, you risk making them feeling disconnected from their jobs and not delivering the best results for you and your company.

There is real value, for everyone concerned, in developing *a culture of appreciation* and being actively positive with your employees about their performance — *when it is warranted*. You have to show your employees that you care about them. You have to make a point of acknowledging when they do something right, because that's when they develop trust in your evaluation of them. They'll understand that you see them as people who deserve recognition. And when some aspect of their performance legitimately disappoints you, they're going to be much more open to listening to you and taking your comments to heart. Never forget that you have to show appreciation in ways that go beyond the financial. A simple 'thank you' makes a huge difference — especially when delivered in person. When they achieve something, thank them and celebrate. In my office, we have a bell that's chimed each time someone achieves something of note. Everyone stops for a second and hears about the achievement — and it takes just a minute out of their day to say 'well done' to a colleague and team member. It's a win-win. It creates a great sense of pride for the person whose achievement is being recognised, and it puts a smile on everyone else's face at the same time. If there's good stuff happening, we don't want to hide it! It's acknowledged, celebrated and appreciated by everyone on the team.

So there you have it — my twelve-point winning structure for what an Engaged Employee needs!

A quick word of warning, though: Applying *too much* structure can stifle engagement. Support this structure with process but don't allow the process to overwhelm personality — it won't have the desired effect. Use it wisely, however, and you'll start to feel the 'engagement electricity' — and so will your customers!

## GOLDEN RULES / HINTS AND TIPS

*Take my twelve-point winning structure above and share it with your leadership team.* Think about the principles described and how they'll work with your own team members. Use it as a guideline or brainstorming framework. The Engaged Organisation Scorecard is a wonderful way to create a common language and understanding around different levels of engagement.

*Ensure your employees understand what engagement means — to you, to the organisation and, most importantly, to them.* They don't know what they don't know. Even leaders don't truly appreciate the power of engagement. So teach them. Once they understand it, they'll want it. Then it's just a case of introducing the right strategies and support, at both an individual and organisational level, to grow and maintain it.

*Only start the process of engaging your employees when you're ready*. Let employees know that it's happening, ask for their feedback and then act on it. Keep your promises, share what you've learned and celebrate success. One of the reasons many engagement programs fail is that the employees' return on investment is poor. By this I mean, they're often asked to invest lots of time and give considered thought to something that doesn't serve them well at all. Most engagement programs take too long to complete, the findings are not shared swiftly and effectively, and employees' perception is that little or no action results. At Engagement Multiplier we've focused on addressing these common mistakes.

If you want to engage your employees, you must swiftly share the results of your engagement surveys, thank them for their feedback, and take action.

*Ask.* Don't just assume you and your leadership know what engages your employees. Ask them! Better still, if you want one-hundred-percent honesty from your team (and that's the only way to create true engagement), you should establish a process that enables them to provide confidential and anonymous feedback on a regular basis. This ensures you will get an honest result, a true insight into what your team is thinking and feeling.

*Ongoing commitment.* When discussing engagement with your employees, you should clearly state that you and your leadership team are absolutely committed to follow through on agreed initiatives and that you're taking action based on their feedback. Share these actions with your team, but don't overcommit. Find three to five ideas you are going to focus on each quarter. That's twelve to twenty a year, thirty-six to sixty over three years. Can you imagine the difference that would make to your organisation?

*Provide a permanent structure for reviewing and, where possible, scoring engagement with your team on at least a quarterly basis.* The very act of thinking about engagement every ninety days raises engagement levels. It also embeds the concept in the sub-conscious and keeps engagement front of mind with your employees (and indeed with your leadership team).

*Provide feedback.* If you're implementing initiatives to help improve engagement, keep your team connected to progress. The team will want to know, 'Did the initiatives that we implemented work or not work?' The great thing is that if they worked, you can celebrate. If they didn't work, there's no big drama as long as you're reviewing progress on a regular basis. There's an opportunity for fast, corrective action.

*Gamification.* Get your team engaged in raising engagement by turning the process into a game. Businesses that manage this properly, seeking feedback and discussing initiatives to raise engagement, will find their teams taking ownership and independently pushing things forward. Turning engagement into a game creates energy and some healthy competition! At Engagement Multiplier, we do this by focusing on the engagement score to enable our clients to share and play the game of improving it (which you can do, too, using the scorecard).

*Small steps and quick wins.* Our advice is to follow the Japanese principle of 'kaizen'—lots of small, incremental improvements that layer very fast so you can start to build up a track record of success and layer success on success. Layers and quick wins will help keep your employees motivated.

*Simplicity.* Keep it simple. The more complicated you make the process of engaging your employees, the more likely you are to create confusion or even fail. Engagement can be simple — even if it isn't always easy.

*Inclusiveness.* Include everyone. Don't make the same mistake I've seen many business owners make. They think that as long as they engage their top people, their leadership, and their top fee-earners, then the rest will be inspired by that. In fact, quite the opposite is true. Aim to very subtly shift engagement from being a top-down directive to being an organisationally owned issue. People value the opportunity to participate and be heard. Everyone is involved. It's not just someone coming in from the outside with clever ideas telling them what they should do.

*Engaged hiring.* Ensure you only employ engaged people to start with! Recruit through the lens of engagement rather than merely that of experience or technical competency. New recruits will become part of your Engaged Organisation — so make sure they've got batteries included!

*Help your people grow as individuals, not just as employees.* Helping them to grow and achieve their goals both inside and outside of the office only serves to improve engagement — and, as mentioned above, helps the employees to bring their whole selves to work.

*Understand their strengths; don't focus on their weaknesses.* The first page of Tom Rath's best-selling book *StrengthsFinder* states, 'We were tired of living in a world that revolved around fixing our weaknesses. Society's relentless focus on people's shortcomings had turned into a global obsession. What's more, we had discovered that people have several times more potential for growth when they invest energy in developing their strengths instead of correcting their deficiencies.'

Every single member of my team reads Rath's book and at the end of it, takes a short online test to understand their five dominant strengths. We combine this with a Kolbe A™ Index (www.Kolbe.com) to enable both the team members and their respective leaders to identify their strengths — then for everyone's benefit, this is where we focus their attention.

Try it. It works.

---

### Engaged Organisation Action: How Did You Score?

If you're using the Engagement Multiplier Program, you will have already seen how you've scored and the direction you should be taking to improve your score further.

If you're using the book or downloaded Scorecard, go to EngagementMultiplier.com/en-gb/eobook for advice and guidance on actions you can consider taking to improve your score.

---

With the final component of your Engaged Organisation in place — and your employees engaged — engagement spreads outward, impacting everyone who comes into contact with your organisation. And that's what we'll cover in the next chapter.

# Chapter 8

# Engaged Customers... and Relationships

## *A self-multiplying resource*

*'When dealing with people, remember you are not dealing with creatures of logic, but creatures of emotion.'*
—Dale Carnegie—

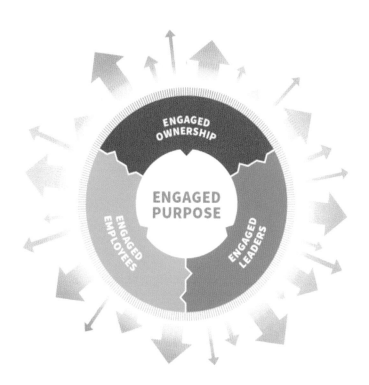

S elf-multiplying resources — that's what every business owner wants! We see growth, profit, productivity, relationships, and revenue — everything that's good about our organisation — growing efficiently and, in some cases, exponentially.

Having read this far, you already appreciate the multiplier effect engagement has on those within your organisation. But it doesn't stop there. Because when you, your purpose, your leaders and employees are all engaged, you'll experience the energy of engagement bursting out beyond the walls of your organisation to the rest of the world. It positively impacts your customers, your suppliers, PR, media, consultants — in fact, anyone who comes into contact with your business. And as a result, they become your organisation's self-multiplying resources. It's an incredibly valuable situation to be in. But there's no need to just take my word for it. Over recent years, numerous surveys and white papers have been written on the topic, as the world realises that Engaged Customers are becoming every organisation's most important competitive advantage.

Companies that engage both their employees and their customers gain a 240 percent boost in performance-related business outcomes. Companies that successfully engage their B2B customers realise sixty-three percent lower customer attrition.

The financial upside of owning an Engaged Organisation is clear both within and outside your business. The internal impact becomes evident first — through more innovation, less waste, fewer work-related accidents, lower absenteeism, improved quality, increased employee retention, and higher productivity levels. The external impact then quickly follows. It's been proven time and time again that Engaged Customers are more loyal, order more frequently, order more products and services, make more referrals, and become some of your most influential brand ambassadors. Your suppliers, consultants, PR, and media all have a choice who they work with, and if you want them to do their best work for you with passion and boundless energy, you need to put clear water between you and your competitors — and you need to engage them too! It's human nature to prioritise work for Engaged Organisations over work for those that aren't. If you're honest, you've probably done it yourself. Have you ever had a choice about whether to work with a business partner you find energising and engaging and one you didn't? Which one did you reach out to first? For which one have you gone the extra mile to keep happy and ensure a positive outcome?

So why, you may ask, are Engaged Customers missing from the Engaged Organisation diagram throughout this book? It's because I passionately believe that you can't truly engage your customers until your organisation itself is engaged. Engaged Customers and other relationships are a by-product of creating, maintaining, and evolving your Engaged Organisation from within. You don't create Engaged Customers; you create an Engaged Organisation and Engaged Customers are the result — a subtle but substantial difference. It's organic, emotional, and ongoing. It's no quick win. It's a long-term state that feeds off the energy your Engaged Organisation transmits. It's not just about attracting new customers. It's about maximising relationships — both at a transactional and emotional level. Nor is it about spending millions of dollars on marketing and advertising. It's about making every touchpoint with your organisation count, because every time someone comes into contact with your business they become either a little more or a little less engaged.

How do you create an Engaged Customer, supplier, consultant, PR person, or media contact? Well, for a start, it's more than creating a 'satisfied' individual. The dictionary definition of the word satisfied is 'to be content or pleased.' In other words, it's what I refer to as 'Successful' on the Engaged Organisation Scorecard: Productive, Conventional Relations. The organisation as a whole attracts and cultivates successful, growth-oriented customers and provides excellent products and services to them. Interaction with customers is businesslike and successful, but sometimes lacks fun, inspiration, and '10× thinking'.

There's nothing wrong with having satisfied customers — in fact, every organisation needs them because they're often the very people who have the potential to become Engaged Customers. But aiming for satisfied customers means you're aspiring to be just the same as the vast majority of business owners. Those are the ones who don't truly appreciate the impact Engaged Customers can have on their organisations. And that's a waste, because they're a real, often untapped, resource.

For many years, focusing on customer satisfaction has been considered a benchmark of success, or the norm. I bet you've taken (and possibly issued) customer satisfaction surveys. Going beyond satisfied and getting your customers engaged gives you a distinct advantage over your competitors. Whilst they have to slash prices, offer special deals and promotions, and run themselves ragged trying to think of news ways to win new business and new customers (let alone keep them), you just need to keep doing what you're doing to reap the rewards of your ROI.

When your customers are engaged, their relationship with your organisation isn't merely transactional, it's emotional — thus making your business more predictable. Yes, you'll still need to seek out new business opportunities and new customers and invest in sustaining them, but when a higher proportion of that new business comes from regular referrals from existing customers and partners, a big part of the sale is already done for you. So ask yourself, why do I want to settle for merely having satisfied customers like everyone else, when I could have Engaged Customers? Do I want my customers to be proud to deal with my organisation — so proud, in fact, they're screaming the virtues of my business from the rooftops?

When you engage your customers, everything grows and everybody wins. Your organisation cares about its customers and passionately, abundantly, and contagiously multiplies its goals to positively impact relationships. It attracts proactive, positive feedback. Customers go the extra mile to nurture the relationship, regularly providing referrals and, in turn, becoming more engaged themselves. Interaction is enjoyable, productive, energising, and often doesn't feel like work.

People are also very forgiving when they're engaged. They'll always look for ways to approve, realising that you're only human. Engaged Customers are more likely to give you latitude when things don't go according to plan. They'll see the bigger picture and value the relationship over the transaction. Never has the need to engage people who come into contact with your business been more important than it is today. Social media means that if you do something great (or badly) for someone, they don't just have the potential to tell a dozen people about it during the course of a conversation or two, they have the potential to tell thousands with a click of a button. Now that's powerful! So powerful, in fact, that it can be a game changer.

So what does it take to develop Engaged Customers?

Well, first and foremost, as mentioned previously, you need to get yourself, your leaders, and employees all engaged before you start focusing on Engaged Customers and other partners. Do a quick Google search and you'll see there's no shortage of stories out there supporting the philosophy that treating your employees well leads to their treating your customers well. And I couldn't agree more. It's the very reason that your purpose is written for your employees and not your customers.

Your customers don't need to know, nor do they frankly care, what your purpose is. They care about their experience of dealing with your organisation, whether you solve a problem they have or supply an enhancement they need. They care about whether what you do makes their lives faster, cheaper, better, easier. They're transacting business with you for a reason — and the reason is that they're expecting a benefit. You need to focus on delivering that benefit to them in a way that's engaging. They are much less concerned about the direction of your business and your plans for the future (although they will, of course, want to know that your business is stable in the short, medium, and longer terms.) If they understand the benefits of an Engaged Organisation, they'll understand it makes your business stronger, more predicable, and more stable even in an unpredictable economic climate. The very experience they receive at the hands of your team will reinforce that.

Engaging your customers takes a team of employees who are successful at connecting what they do functionally to why they do it. It's about the employees truly connecting the customer to your purpose — not by simply expressing it in corporate communications, but by how they make the customer feel, by making an emotional connection. It's the cascade effect I've mentioned in previous chapters. Your purpose connects with your employees at an emotional level — and in turn, your Engaged Employees connect with your customers at an emotional level as well.

This emotional connection means that when people contact your organisation, your team does more than just make a sale, deal with a customer inquiry, or organise one of your suppliers. It means your customers and partners feel like the person they're dealing with cares and will do everything within their power to make them feel valued. They feel that your team wants to build and maintain mutually rewarding relationships where both they (the customer) and your employee enjoy an energising interaction.

Engaged Customers feed off Engaged Employees and vice-versa. When the phone rings, there's no sigh or 'look, here comes more work'; there's a smile that says, 'I really love speaking with you' — and people feel that warmth and energy through your verbal, face-to-face, and written interactions. Customers feel there's a difference when compared to other companies offering the same products and services. They do more than just look at your products; they base their judgment on how they feel about the time they spend in your 'company'.

One of the things I was taught very early on by the Strategic Coach Program is to **systematise the predictable and humanise the**

**exceptional**. Creating engagement with your customers (and indeed your team) also often means creating unexpected outcomes; your organisation goes above and beyond a normal efficient transactional process of providing a product or service (i.e., creating a 'satisfied customer'). You can create customer *service* by being really well organised and efficient, but to create an engaging customer *experience* normally requires the customer to feel something good happened that they didn't expect. You can really have fun with this, as there's no shortage of ways to create the unexpected if you think carefully and creatively. Here's an example from my consulting firm in the UK. One of my team, Susie, meets and greets all our customers when they visit our offices. My consulting firm's customers are highly successful business owners and entrepreneurs, who are used to being greeted very efficiently by the many organisations they come into contact with.

However, they often make positive reference to the way that Susie welcomes them on arrival, because it's done in ways they don't expect. She'll personalise a parking space for them; when they enter the boardroom the first thing they see is the personal welcome message she's placed on the plasma screen; she offers them a choice of fifteen different beverages, some of which she's spent her own time sourcing on the weekends. She does it with a smile on her face and in her eyes. She makes a real effort, and it shows. It's not just efficient, it feels personal and genuine, and that's because it is — Susie's engaged. People really appreciate it and, dare I say, find it engaging!

When your employees are engaged with your customers at an emotional level, they'll also know when things are right and when they aren't. If, for some reason, things aren't going according to plan, your team will be inspired and motivated and find innovative ways to turn potentially negative or damaging situations into positive outcomes. The emotional connection develops a sense of personal responsibility that your Engaged Employees happily rise to the challenge of meeting. John Pepper, CEO and co-founder of Boloco, told his employees: 'You are allowed to do this... don't worry about the rules and don't worry about getting into trouble. Your job is to take care of the customer. Your job is to make the person leave happy.'

Here's a recent example of when I became an Engaged Customer. In 2015, my wife Diana and I visited the St. Regis Hotel in Abu Dhabi. Our whole stay was a joy, but there's one particular experience I will never forget.

On the second night of our stay, we went to the hotel bar and met a member of staff named Eloy. I ordered a cigar, and we got talking. It was clear we both shared a passion for cigars. He mentioned that, just a few days before our arrival, a lady from Cuba had hosted a hand-rolling cigar demonstration at the hotel, which had proved to be a great experience. I enquired whether she was due to return to the hotel and, to my disappointment, the answer was no. However, Eloy immediately offered to take it upon himself to find out if there would be an opportunity to see her at another hotel.

He went on to find out that she was due to host the same event the following day at a hotel about 20 miles away from the St. Regis. Excited, I asked the concierge to arrange tickets, only to find it was sold out.

It's fair to say that I was a little disappointed. That evening, Diana and I had dinner at the hotel and during our meal a member of staff approached me with a small bag. In the bag were an envelope and a box. The envelope contained a handwritten note from Eloy. It said that he was sorry to learn that I wasn't able to make the event and that he had enclosed a gift. In the box was not only one of the hand-rolled cigars the lady had been making, but also one of my favourite cigars; Eloy had obviously been listening to me when we were talking about cigars during our first meeting. I was genuinely overwhelmed!

After dinner we went to the bar to thank Eloy. I asked him, 'Where did you get the cigar?' His response was, 'When the lady hosted the hand-rolling experience last week, she gave us all a cigar, and this is the one she gave me. When I learned you couldn't attend her event tomorrow, I asked my manager for permission to go home and get it, so I could give it to you. Knowing how passionate you are about cigars, I thought you would appreciate it more.'

I was absolutely gobsmacked. What an incredibly generous gesture. I smoked the cigar. It was incredible. So, on arrival back in the UK, I bought some of my favourite cigars and sent them to Eloy. I also wrote to the manager of the hotel to express my gratitude and genuine delight at Eloy's efforts to go the extra mile to engage their guests.

If you can create the same type of experience for your clients, they will feel the same way I feel about the St. Regis Hotel — a raving fan who was genuinely touched by the way in which Eloy handled a situation. It's an experience I won't forget, and I've since recommended the St. Regis to numerous friends. So yes, the St. Regis has another Engaged Customer and, indeed, a self-multiplying resource in me!

## GOLDEN RULES / HINTS AND TIPS

*Focus on the inside first.* Engage your leaders and employees first. They're the people who deal with your customers, suppliers, PR, media, and consultants day in and day out, so they're the people who have the power to make or break engagement with everyone outside the organisation.

*Test understanding.* Ensure your leaders and employees (new and existing) understand and appreciate what it means to engage a customer and how what they do impacts customer engagement. Also remember, if your employees are only engaged at a transactional level, your customers will only be as well.

*Release untapped potential.* Look at your existing customers — think about who is engaged and who isn't. Which of your customers do you consider merely satisfied that has the potential to be engaged if they're not already? Are you doing enough to keep your customers engaged, or have you and your team become complacent? Then ask yourself, what are you going to do about it?

*Woo them, and keep wowing them! Show your customers that you care.* Customers need to be wooed continually. If you're going to keep a customer engaged, don't take him or her for granted. If you aren't paying ongoing special attention to your customers, the simple reality is that someone else will! There are little things you can do to show customers they aren't just another box that needs to be checked. It can be something as simple as sending them a handwritten thank-you note; we all love receiving them, they make us feel appreciated, and they are one of those unexpected outcomes I mentioned earlier.

There's a phrase I'm sure you've heard many times: 'It's the thought that counts.' I remember a time in the very early days of my consulting business, as the holiday season was approaching. It was when I only had a small number of clients. I thoughtfully created a cocktail set for each customer that included special glasses, a handmade cocktail shaker, cocktail recipes, and all the ingredients to make a few drinks. At the same time, my competitors (in the main large private banks) were taking clients to expensive sporting events and corporate hospitality events with budgets that were way out of my league. The events were also a little impersonal, with hosting and organisation outsourced to third parties.

I'm sharing this story because one of the recipients of the cocktail set reminded me of it — nearly 20 years later! It showed him we cared beyond simply putting our hands in our pockets — the thought counted!

*Ask them.* Your customers may have more day-to-day contact with various aspects of your organisation than you do. So if you want to know how they feel about your organisation, ask them. They will be deeply touched — everyone wants to be asked for their opinion, and yet this happens so infrequently.

My experience working with our customers at Engagement

Multiplier continually reinforces how much learning and growth can be gained by listening to your customers' feedback. Remember, if they're engaged, they care, and if they care, they're happy to provide feedback. The important thing, however, is to know when to ask for that feedback.

At Engagement Multiplier, we're developing a module that elegantly enables your organisation to reach out and connect with your best customers and partners and have them score how engaged they believe your organisation is. They can also provide feedback, guidance, and advice. It's a great way to connect with your best customers and obtain valuable insight. Importantly, however, we only make this facility available to Engagement Multiplier customers when they've maintained engaged status in each area of the Engaged Organisation Scorecard for a sustained period of time.

We restrict access to this module until then because, as stated above, until your own house is in order, you can't truly engage your customers. You're so much better off asking for customer feedback from a position of security and strength, when you know the internal resources are engaged and ready to start receiving feedback — and more importantly, to act upon it. Taking this 360 approach not only makes your customers feel even more connected and invested in their relationship with you, it provides your organisation with another opportunity to achieve its Engaged Purpose.

**Share feedback.** If you're going to get feedback from your customers to help your business become more engaged, you must share the results and dignify their feedback by providing details of the actions you're going to take. Then, in the same way you have to take action so that everyone in the business knows you're serious about engagement, you have to demonstrate the same to your customers. They also then feel that their investment and commitment to providing feedback has been worthwhile — that's *their* ROI. It's also equally important to share any feedback provided by your customers with your employees; they are, after all, the people on the front line whose actions have largely dictated the responses you've received.

*Go the extra mile to nurture the relationship.* Tap into the basic desire of human beings to bond with those around them. People don't just want to do business; they want to make friends with you. Let them! It will make business so much more rewarding (and possibly fun) for both of you! I remember this great quotation from Roger Staubach, legendary American football quarterback of the Dallas Cowboys, after Super Bowl VI: 'There are no traffic jams along the extra mile.'

*Make interaction enjoyable, productive, and energising so it doesn't feel like work.* Become the company your customers dream about and want to keep. Tony Robbins likes to tell business audiences, 'You guys don't work for a living. Work is digging ditches and breaking roads. What you do for a living is make friends!' So remember that whatever business you think you're in, you're really in the friend-making business!

*Call out the exceptional and celebrate.* Calling out the exceptional behaviours that create wonderful moments with customers (as Eloy did with me) and celebrating them with your team helps provide context for everyone else as to what the exceptional looks like. If you call these out appropriately, it will reinforce the behaviours that created the experience and encourage more of the same behaviour as well as providing great examples for recognition and engagement!

*Take your time.* Engaging your employees doesn't happen overnight or through a one-off action, and engaging customers is no different. It takes time, and some will need more convincing than others. But with continued focus, thoughtful action, and follow-through on feedback, your customers will become engaged.

*Stay in the zone.* Bottling the 'engagement energy' is one thing. Maintaining your supply is another. Regular, ongoing focus is essential not only to engaging your customers but to magnifying the impact they have on your organisation — and you can't sustain Engaged Customers if you're not continuously focusing on keeping your own organisation engaged. Stay in the zone.

---

**Engaged Organisation Action: How Did You Score?**

If you're using the Engagement Multiplier Program, you will have already seen how you've scored and the direction you should be taking to improve your score further.

If you're using the book or downloaded Scorecard, go to EngagementMultiplier.com/en-gb/eobook for advice and guidance on actions you can consider taking to improve your score.

---

There's a mindset shift that occurs when you stop thinking that it's just customers who are, or have the potential to be, self-multiplying resources for your organisation. Nurturing relationships with anyone who comes into contact with your business not only makes your organisation more successful, predictable, and energising, it makes business easier because you view everyone you interact with through the lens of engagement. And when you do that, you get to build the 'company' you dream about!

# Chapter 9

# The Company You Dream About

## *Mastery of the magic*

*'Why wait to be memorable?'*
—Tony Robbins—

Congratulations! By reading this far you now have all the information you need to start creating your own Engaged Organisation.

You now know what an Engaged Organisation looks like and why it's so important. You have, right at your very fingertips, the structure, framework, golden rules, and suggested strategies for actions you can take to not only raise engagement but to maintain and multiply it within your organisation — and beyond.

Having an Engaged Organisation isn't just about having a business that's more productive, more profitable, and growing faster. It's more than that. It's about you and your team becoming united around a common Engaged Purpose that inspires and motivates you all, which in turn delivers an outstanding experience for you, your team, and your customers — in fact, anyone who comes into contact with your organisation. An Engaged Organisation is one that's filled with energised, happy people, all fulfilling their potential, and as a result, you and your organisation fulfil yours. It truly is the company you dream about, one that is committed, connected, and comprises engaged people who 'own' engagement and strive to continuously improve it. The energy produced by an Engaged Organisation is palpable — lifting everyone to new heights both personally and professionally.

I started this book by writing: 'Engagement is magical. More specifically, the outcomes delivered by engagement are magical. In the same way an accomplished magician delivers an extraordinary outcome that delights and astonishes, engagement transforms both lives and businesses from ordinary to extraordinary.' So, why wait to create magic? What are you waiting for?

It's now time to turn learning into meaningful action so you and your team — in fact, anyone who comes into contact with your organisation — experience something extraordinary.

As a reader of this book, you're clearly connected to the idea of creating an Engaged Organisation. My view is that if you're going to do something in life, do it really well. In other words, as the expression says, 'If you're going to be a bear, be a grizzly.'

To create the company you dream about is not about taking half measures. I was taught many years ago that the only place that success comes before work is in the dictionary. To create an exceptional Engaged Organisation is going to take some commitment on your part. But as you've seen in this book, the steps are straightforward. It takes courage and bravery to be an Engaged Owner — which is why I love the quote about bears.

It's time for you now to commit to engagement and for it to not just be a fad or a phase. For you to pull this off and create the company you dream about requires openness, honesty, and an acceptance of the fact that you have to listen to your team. You have to act on their feedback, and you have to be willing as the owner to be scored yourself in terms of your own personal levels of engagement. As Dan Sullivan said shortly after his organisation began using Engagement Multiplier, 'The fact that my team is grading me makes me show up in the right way.' It's often the small things that make the big differences.

Start with what I've shared with you in these chapters. You will build a wonderful business. Your employees, moreover, will remember you for far more than the money you pay them whilst they work for you.

That's really magical to me, and I hope it is for you, too. As I like to say: It's one thing to be a successful entrepreneur; it's something entirely different to be a *legendary* entrepreneur. So as a famous TV starship captain often said, 'Engage!' And you'll find yourself light-years ahead of your competition.

No doubt, as you experience the joys and benefits of running an Engaged Organisation, you'll join an elite group I refer to as 'The Engagement Multipliers'.

In the next chapter, I'll explain who they are.

Chapter 10

# The Engagement Multipliers

*Share your story and engage others*

*'If your actions inspire others to dream more, learn more,*
*do more, and become more, you are a leader.'*
—John Quincy Adams—

As I'm sure you've already gathered, I'm really passionate about engagement! I love the impact it has on businesses and individuals, and I'm on something of a crusade to help over 100 million people become measurably more engaged.

And nothing makes people sit up and listen more than hearing or reading about real-life stories of success. It is motivating to learn about actual people who have achieved impressive results and operate with an abundance mindset; who are happy to share their insights, knowledge, experience, and advice with others; and who, in the process, inspire people to follow their example and achieve their own levels of greater success. Such stories have been a source of incredible learning for me over many years — both through our 'Engagement Multipliers' and through my reading of many articles about and autobiographies from the world's greatest innovators and thought leaders.

As you experience the benefits and rewards of engagement and building an Engaged Organisation, I'd love to hear from you so that I can share your story with others. I am publishing a series of books called 'The Engagement Multipliers'. Each book will contain twelve chapters, each dedicated to an Engaged Organisation and business owner who will share the approaches and actions they've taken that have had a positive or even profound impact on their levels of engagement, their business, and everyone within it.

The process is simple (and dare I say engaging!). One of our team will contact you, conduct a short interview, and send the chapter to you for approval. It will cost you nothing, and as an 'Engagement Multiplier' you'll appreciate the benefits and practical uses in your own branding and marketing efforts — as well as provide a huge pat on the back for your engaged team!

Everyone loves working with and for Engaged Organisations — so if you have one, don't keep it a secret. Become an Engagement Multiplier, share your story, and help inspire the world to become more engaged!

# Acknowledgements

This book has been more than two years in the making, and it's been quite a journey. I've moved through various stages of edits, writing, and rewriting, and I can't express just how thankful I am for everybody involved, every step of the way.

In particular, Jayne Deakin deserves a very special mention. She has devoted more time than she would care to remember, helping me structure my thoughts and find the right words. She was heavily involved in constructing both chapters and insights, and quite frankly, this book would not exist but for her unrelenting support. Jayne has worked with me for many years and has a fabulous unique ability of being able to 'connect the dots'. Drawing from our experience of working with clients and Engagement Multipliers, she came up with valuable content that I probably would have missed if left alone to write. Her contribution was of such significance that I wanted to name her as a co-author. Preferring to be out of the spotlight, she politely declined. This book was very much a joint effort, though, and I am very grateful and fortunate that I had her help.

I'm also grateful to the many Engagement Multiplier clients and engaged team members who constantly provide me with such inspiration and valuable insight. I will never tire of learning about the innovative ways they improve engagement levels and the wonderful stories that result. Please don't stop building those fabulous businesses where people love to work.

Martin and Brigitte Skan, for their belief in not just me, but the Engagement Multiplier business itself. Your support has been invaluable and enabled me to accelerate making our platform available to the world. Thank you both — and keep up the youthful exuberance!

My team, who pushed me to get this book done and who spent all these months on it, giving me hours of their time, supporting me, and enabling us to build and launch Engagement Multiplier. In particular,

Todd Brook, an exceptional entrepreneur and leader whom I feel very fortunate to work with and have leading our US operations.

Last, but by no means least, my wife Diana, who has consistently stood by me — even when things got really tough on the entrepreneurial journey. Her constant support and belief in me is remarkable. I am most fortunate.

The time, effort, and energy that went into putting together a book, whilst also building and launching a digital engagement platform, was a little overwhelming at times. That we managed both successfully is quite incredible. And that every single person stuck by me, and saw it through, is even more incredible. I couldn't be more grateful.

# About the Author

Stefan Wissenbach is an entrepreneur, speaker, and best-selling author. He has helped hundreds of companies improve culture, profitability, and productivity, whilst becoming happier places to work — all through the transformational power of engagement.

Stefan has committed the next twenty-five years of his life to help over 100 million people become measurably more engaged.

He is the founder of EngagementMultiplier.com, a global exponential company that enables businesses anywhere in the world to measure and improve engagement levels every ninety days. More than eighty percent of Engagement Multiplier's clients achieve 'Engaged' status in less than twelve months, enabling business owners and entrepreneurs to pursue their vision and passion with confidence — and build self-multiplying organisations.

His books, businesses, and speaking engagements provide education and inspiration to enable businesses and individuals fulfil their potential and bridge the gap between aspiration and achievement. His unique 'uncommon' common-sense approach is to simplify the complex and provide a framework for people to take action, distilling a lifetime of learning into simple success strategies that anyone can master.

His first book, *Slaying Dragons & Moving Mountains*, focuses on simple ways for individuals to become more engaged and achieve personal success, whilst his Nightingale Conant audio program, *Your Magic Future*, provides the formula for individuals to make work optional. In addition, he is the co-author of *Change Agents* with Brian Tracy and *Think & Grow Rich Today*.

For over twenty years, he has been a leading adviser to successful entrepreneurs. He is the creator of The Magic Number®, the Founder of MagicFuture.com, and the co-founder of The Magic Future Foundation.

Stefan is married with three children and lives in Warwickshire, England.

To order copies of this book or provide feedback, please visit:

EngagementMultiplier.com/en-gb/eobook

Made in the USA
Columbia, SC
09 September 2017